ELTON WELSBY

Game For A Laugh

ELTON WELSBY

WITH GARY COOK

ELTON WELSBY

Publisher Curly Fish Ltd.

128 City Road
London
EC1V 2NX
United Kingdom

Copyright © 2024 Elton Welsby and Curly Fish Ltd.

All rights reserved.

ISBN: 979-8-3012-5103-0

A BIG THANKS

I'd like to dedicate this book to my children, Chris and Laura, my two grandsons, Dylan and Oscar and my family in St. Helens.

I'd also like to thank John Charlton for allowing the use of the photo on the cover, featuring his dad Jack.

I can't forget my two old mates Richard Keys and Andy Gray either. The moment I said I was going to do the book, they both agreed to do the foreword. Cheers both of you!

Gary would like to dedicate the book to his wife Heather and two daughters Sophie and Amélie. He would also like to thank his parents Pete and Diane. A special mention also goes to the Clarke family - Mick, Eileen and David.

ELTON WELSBY

CONTENTS

Foreword by Richard Keys and Andy Gray   9

Introduction   12

Chapter 1 Falling in love with the game   15

Chapter 2 The Shakespeare Club   27

Chapter 3 Meeting Mr Shankly   35

Chapter 4 Radio City   44

Chapter 5 Taking the Mic   53

Chapter 6 Friends not Foes   61

Chapter 7 Bruges   68

Chapter 8 The road to Rome   72

Chapter 9 From Rome to Manchester   78

Chapter 10 A face for TV   86

Chapter 11 Goodbye Bill   96

Chapter 12 Espana 82   104

Chapter 13 Bob and Brian   112

Chapter 14 Bowled over   118

Chapter 15 The Renaissance   125

Chapter 16 Saints alive   132

Chapter 17 If I can dream   139

Chapter 18 What a result   145

Chapter 19 Mexico 86   151

Chapter 20 A good sport   161

Chapter 21 Euro 88   167

Chapter 22 I know you got Seoul   175

Chapter 23 Never a dull Sunday	185
Chapter 24 Hillsborough	196
Chapter 25 Up for grabs	198
Chapter 26 Italia 90	204
Chapter 27 None shall sleep	210
Chapter 28 The perfect match	217
Chapter 29 The final season	224
Chapter 30 Euro 92	230
Chapter 31 Back home	237
Chapter 32 Holes not goals	242
Chapter 33 On the road again	250
Chapter 34 Balls up	257
Chapter 35 Full circle	264
Chapter 36 The last laugh	272
Chapter 37 The last word	279

FOREWORD

BY RICHARD KEYS AND ANDY GRAY

First, Richard.

Elton Welsby is one of the best sports anchors the UK has ever seen. Make no mistake about that. He was doing things in our business long before anyone else. And he did them very well.

Elton was the little guy from the North West who packed a mighty punch. He was too good to ignore. He was a fine football anchor – one of the first to operate without the crutch of autocue.

All of this will become evident as you read the book. It's a long overdue publication and will help you to understand how different the media world once was.

It wasn't long after joining Liverpool's independent radio station – Radio City – that I found myself in Elton's back garden, helping to put up a swing for his children Christopher and Laura. I now work with Christopher.

I've often wondered why I didn't leave the odd screw loose!

Elton took me on a night out by way of a thank you and gave me some of the best advice I've ever had – "Never use autocue, it's too restricting". As the new kid operating in a patch he'd made his own, he always had time for me.

I'm looking forward to reading the book myself. Elton worked in an era that was so much more trusting than now.

An era when you could go for dinner with a player twice in the same week – once with his girlfriend and the other time with his wife.

An era when players could trash a hotel when away on a retreat – but no-one would report the incident.

An era when a rival reporter would file his mate's copy because he was too pissed to do it himself.

An era when opportunities were few and far between, so you had to be good to stand out.

Elton stood out.

He mixed it with some of the finest of that era and there are going to be tales galore to follow in this book.

Imagine being as close to Shankly as Elton was.

Now over to Andy.

After moving down from Scotland at a very young age to play most of my career in England, I watched Elton become a household name in the UK alongside the likes of Saint and Greavsie, Jimmy Hill, Des Lynam and other giants of sports broadcasting.

However, it was after my move to Everton in 1983 when I got to know him personally and professionally.

After years of sitting in studios myself, it's still impressive to see the best broadcasters maintain a level of calmness live on air while it's all kicking off behind the scenes. Elton was one of the very best at it.

Being an Evertonian, the North West and in particular Merseyside, was his manor. Supporters of both Everton and Liverpool saw him as one of their own, forging a career that took him to national fame while never leaving the area.

Finally, I can't talk about Elton without mentioning one of mine and Goodison's greatest ever nights.

24th April 1985

Everton 3 Bayern Munich 1.

An atmosphere I nor anyone else there will forget.

Fittingly, at full time the first person I saw in the tunnel was Elton with his microphone. It was an incredible night in an incredible era for Everton and it was great to share those moments with a fellow Blue.

INTRODUCTION

Summer 1992

Football is about to change forever. The Premier League is about to be launched and Sky TV have the rights to show the live games. As part of the deal, the BBC have Match of the Day to show highlights every Saturday night.

I work for ITV. Since 1988, the channel has had exclusivity of top-flight English football.

I'm the main presenter of "The Match". Every Sunday I appear on your screens. I introduce the live game. I talk to my guest. It could be Brian Clough, George Best, Alex Ferguson, maybe Bobby Robson. Then I pass over to the commentator, usually the great Brian Moore.

Not anymore.

ITV have nothing. They lost.

And I have no idea what's going on. You see, I'm in Sweden for ITV's coverage of the European Championship. My life is about to change but I'm oblivious to it all.

I've been paired with Jack Charlton, World Cup winner with England in 1966 and current manager of Ireland. With the Irish narrowly missing out on qualification, Jack has been free to work with us on the tournament. We've been together for the whole thing.

The viewers enjoy his insight, his warm personality. He's a big hit. But nobody benefits more than me from being in the presence of Jack Charlton in Sweden. Of all the ex-players and managers that I worked with, I feel as close to Jack as any of them.

After the final of Euro 92, which saw Denmark beat Germany, Big Jack and I decide to head for a drink. One last tipple before we head back home.

Jack has a World Cup campaign to prepare for. My career is about to go in a different direction. We've worked hard throughout Euro 92. We deserve this one last drink or two.

The bar is busy and there's an atmosphere building. I leave Jack for a minute to go to the toilet. As I'm relieving myself a large German asks me a question:

"Are you Danish?"

I tell him I'm English.

Next minute, I'm in a heap on the ground. The end of a wonderful few weeks has come to this. I'm on a Swedish toilet floor, out cold.

I start to come round. All I can smell is piss.

I'm groggy. Sweden has been great. But now this. Everything I've worked for, every game I've covered, every mile I've travelled. My last night before I go home to my family.

Back in England, my future is being discussed by ITV bosses. I won't find out what's in store for me for a few days yet.

Jack has no idea what's happened. He's looking around the bar for me. I'm not easy to find. He's Big Jack. Nobody ever called me Big Elton.

I gingerly make my way back to him. He sees my face.

"What the fook happened to you?"

I can't let it spoil things. It hurts to smile and I look like shit. Jack makes sure I'm ok. The next day we say our goodbyes. By now the swelling on my face has really come out.

He looks at me, shakes his head and then my hand.

"See you soon kid."

I know that it won't be long before we're back together again. I just don't know when it will be. I'm at a career crossroads but I'm very lucky. I've been living my dream since the early 1970s.

So how did it all happen?

Well, my love of football all started in a Cheshire town in the late 1950s.

1

Falling in love with the game

Being a kid in the 1950s was nothing like it is today. Technology was limited and the knock-on effect from the Second World War was still being felt. It was a time when the smallest gesture felt huge.

And that's how I fell in love with football.

I was born in St. Helens on Merseyside in 1951, a large town that's famous for another sport; rugby league. It wasn't until we moved to Macclesfield in Cheshire that my passion began.

My dad was a senior figure at a local bank in the town. And it's during that time, I was introduced to football.

At the age of seven, my dad started taking me to watch Macclesfield Town. The club played at the Moss Rose ground and were in the Cheshire League. They'd later play as high as the third tier of English football at the end of the 20th century, but they were a long way from that back in the late 1950s.

I loved going there. It didn't matter what level they were or how small the ground was. For me, it felt enormous. I had nothing to compare it to, of course. I was going to the games with my dad. That was the most important thing.

One day the club invited some of the local kids to walk out with the players.

Each child entered the field by the side of one of the Macclesfield players. Little did I know, the man stood next to me, tightly clasping my little hand, was the former England international Neil Franklin.

Franklin's career was coming to a close, but he'd been a great player at Stoke City and played with the legendary Sir Stanley Matthews. He became infamous when he left

England to play in Colombia in 1950. It was considered a hugely controversial move at the time.

The financial package offered to go to Bogota was almost impossible to turn down. The decision ended his international hopes and he was back on home soil just a few months later. Franklin found himself suspended by Stoke and then sold. He'd never play for England again.

With football now in my blood, another opportunity arose to watch more games when dad was promoted to the position of bank manager in Liverpool. We moved to the city and the seeds were planted for life as an Evertonian.

It's only a small segment of this book, and of course it plays a part in the grand scheme of things, but writing about modern Everton is no laughing matter. So I've taken the decision not to.

In the spring of 1962, my dad came to me with a simple question:

"Would you like to go and watch football this Saturday?"

My eyes lit up. Of course I did.

"Are we going to watch Macclesfield Dad?"

"No, I'm taking you to Anfield. We're going to a Liverpool game."

This wasn't the Cheshire League. This was Liverpool, playing at home. But we were naïve and fate stepped in and stopped it happening.

We were so used to turning up at Macclesfield Town and paying at the turnstiles. Dad thought we could do the same to watch Liverpool.

It was impossible.

The place was packed and we couldn't get in. I stood there outside the stadium and watched as the chance disappeared. The turnstiles were closed. I was devastated.

The experience at Anfield led to my dad getting tickets for the Everton vs. Cardiff City game at Goodison Park shortly afterwards. He didn't want us to go through that again.

Dad wasn't going to take any risks. One of his customers, Sydney Moss, kindly helped us, despite being on the board of directors at Liverpool.

On 28th April 1962, I watched the Blues for the very first time.

And what a game!

Everton hammered Cardiff 8-3 in the final home match of the season. I was instantly in love with this team. They were brilliant. I had a new hero too; "The Golden Vision" Alex Young. He was amazing and I was hooked.

Everton were managed by Harry Catterick, who'd done a great job at Sheffield Wednesday before replacing Johnny Carey at Goodison Park in April 1961.

The decision was an unpopular one; Carey was well liked by the supporters and the manner of his sacking left a bitter taste.

Chairman John Moores took Carey for a taxi ride and dismissed him during the journey. Now you know where the expression "taxi for…" comes from when a manager is about to get the boot.

Despite having a good record at his old club, Catterick had to convince the Everton fans he was the right man for the job. Many still felt aggrieved by the departure of Carey.

When midfielder Bobby Collins left the club in 1962 for Leeds United, there was more disgruntlement on the terraces. Dennis Stevens, the cousin of Duncan Edwards, arrived from Bolton. Stevens was another who needed to win over the supporters.

His crime? Not being Bobby Collins.

In Catterick's first full season, Everton finished fourth. Building on this, the following year we were in a title race.

The favourites were Spurs, and honestly, they were brilliant. Spurs had won the league and FA Cup double in 1961. It was the first time it'd been done in the 20th century.

Their manager Bill Nicholson had built an excellent team of players including Danny Blanchflower, Cliff Jones and John White and then added Jimmy Greaves, as Spurs retained the cup at Wembley in 1962.

The deciding moment of the season came when Tottenham arrived at Goodison Park in April 1963. We were third, with Spurs one place higher by virtue of goal average. Leicester City were leading the way with a one-point advantage.

It's from this match that I have one of my greatest memories. The game was only seventeen minutes old when Roy Vernon ran down the wing. He crossed into the Tottenham penalty area where Young was up against Maurice Norman. It was a complete mismatch. He was so much taller than Young.

I can still see it now. I've replayed this moment in my head so many times.

Young rose and seemed to hang in the air. He stayed there while Norman came back down to earth. "The Golden Vision" met the ball and headed it home.

Goodison Park erupted. I'm getting goosebumps thinking about it.

It proved to be the winner too. The 1-0 victory gave Everton further momentum and took them into first place. Everton won their final four matches. A 4-1 victory over Fulham confirmed the title with Roy Vernon scoring a hat trick.

Everton were the champions of England.

What a time to be a Blue!

Just days after the league campaign ended, Spurs won the European Cup Winners' Cup in Rotterdam by thrashing Atletico Madrid 5-1. They were the first English club to lift a European trophy.

The 1963/64 season saw the Shankly-inspired Liverpool win the league and, a year later, the FA Cup.

Twelve months on, it was Everton's turn to reach Wembley. The league season had been disappointing. We finished eleventh. Liverpool were champions again.

The cup run breathed life into everyone at Goodison Park. The semi-final was held at Burden Park, home of Bolton Wanderers. Manchester United stood in our way.

A 0-0 draw was on the cards until a young midfielder called Colin Harvey popped up to put Everton in the final with just over ten minutes to go.

When Colin's goal went in, the Everton end went crazy. I was in the middle of it all. Someone threw me in the air. I'm not the biggest of blokes so I took off quite easily.

Thankfully, on the way down another supporter managed to catch me before I hit someone or something. I don't know who it was. But without him, this book might not have been possible!

Younger fans will find it hard to understand what the final meant to the country. It didn't matter who was playing, everyone watched it. It was one of the most popular days of the year.

Then my dad hit me with a bombshell. I couldn't go to Wembley for the game, I was too young. Luckily my cousin

Terry stepped forward and said he'd take me. My dad caved in.

Wednesday had a two-goal lead just before the hour. Everton's hopes were in tatters. We thought about leaving and going home. We decided to stick it out and thank God we stayed. Two minutes after Wednesday's second, we were back in it. And it came from an unlikely source.

Most of us were disappointed that Fred Pickering hadn't been picked by Harry Catterick. His place went to Mike Trebilcock and we couldn't understand why.

Trebilcock had hardly played all season, even if he did get a run out in the semi-final. But now Trebilcock had given us hope. Five minutes later and Trebilcock scored again to level up the game. He certainly justified his selection.

Who were we to doubt our manager? What did we know?

We'd been dead and buried. Derek Temple made it 3-2 in the 74th minute, capping off a comeback that only began a quarter of an hour before. Everton had won the FA Cup in dramatic fashion.

What a moment!

Later that year of course England won the World Cup. I remember watching the final but it wasn't as big of a deal as it would be today. Perhaps it was my age. It's likely that I didn't grasp the whole situation or what it meant.

To complete some great football memories of 1966, I made a trip to Anfield because Ajax were in town for a European Cup game against Liverpool. I wanted to see Johan Cruyff play. That was the only reason. I'd heard about the first leg and this guy I had to see.

Was he as good as they said?

Guided by Dutch genius Rinus Michels, Ajax destroyed the Reds 5-1 in Amsterdam. Prior to the second leg, Bill

Shankly boldly declared that Liverpool would score at least seven.

He was totally wrong.

Ajax drew first blood through Cruyff. He'd already scored in the first game, now he'd killed the tie. Roger Hunt made it 1-1, but Cruyff got a second. Hunt equalised once more but Liverpool were out 7-3 on aggregate.

It was a pleasure to have seen Johan Cruyff in the flesh for the first time. As I walked away from Anfield, raving about this exciting young Dutchman, little did I know that he was also a gentleman.

I'd find that out later on.

It wasn't always easy watching Everton play. My school had compulsory games on a Saturday afternoon. We had to do lessons in the morning, followed by sport later on.

There were three different possibilities. One was rugby with our coach Alan Ashcroft. He'd played for England and the British Lions. He was the rugby master and also taught art. There was cross country and hockey as well. You had to do one of them.

So the plan was simple; skip all three in order to watch Everton.

Along with my friend Tony Wadsworth, we bunked off to go to Goodison Park. While we were watching Everton, the rugby guys thought we were hockey training. The hockey lads figured we must be doing cross country.

Most of the time it worked. We got caught out twice.

Corporal punishment was still a thing in schools and so the cane was waiting for us on both occasions. We got a good whacking on the backside.

Six times!

Our headmaster, Mr Collison, was an intimidating figure and we feared and respected him. Oddly, he often had his dog, a labrador called Rudy, with him.

The first time we got caught, we were in Mr Collison's office waiting to take our medicine.

As we bent over, the headmaster lifted the cane and Rudy thought it was a game. He started to bark and jumped into the air. He wanted to grab that stick! I wish he had. Our arses were black and blue after six lashings.

Naturally, the other kids wanted to see the proof, so we had to show them the bruises. There were some serious marks and those scars stayed for a while.

Everyone cheered and laughed when we got our arses out, but there was no funny side for me or Tony. The only positive from our beating was that we got to see Everton play.

The punishment was a painful experience. But it didn't put us off. When we were reprimanded again, we put padding down the backs of our trousers to try and reduce the impact.

It worked. There wasn't a single mark. Again, we had to prove it to the rest of the lads. They couldn't believe it when we didn't have one trace of the cane.

Everton made it to Wembley once more for the 1968 FA Cup final. I couldn't go. Thank goodness. West Brom nicked it with a Jeff Astle goal.

With World Cup winner Alan Ball established in the side along with Harvey and Howard Kendall, Everton came third in 1969.

The three players were known as the "Holy Trinity" at Goodison Park and they worked so well together. It was like they had a telepathic connection.

We were hopeful of yet another FA Cup final appearance too. A group of us set off to Villa Park for the semi-final against league champions Manchester City in our battered old car. It wasn't to be. A late Tommy Booth goal sent City to Wembley.

It was a very sombre mood in the car on the way back. Hardly a word was spoken until our four-wheel wreck was overtaken by a coach.

It was the Everton team bus.

Expecting to see the players in a similar mood to ourselves, we were somewhat taken aback to see them passing round the champagne and having a good laugh.

No doubt it was gallows humour and the champagne was planned for a different outcome. What made it worse we didn't even have a can of lager between us.

Que sera sera.

It's at this time that I was about to start my second job. Yes, second! After leaving school, I worked at an insurance company. I hated it. I was so happy to leave. I have nothing nice to say about the year that I worked there.

My next job was completely different.

Not long afterwards, I became a porter at Liverpool's Broadgreen Hospital. The role was nothing like it is today, I had to do a variety of tasks. Some of them were extremely unpleasant. Dead bodies and regular trips to the morgue were part and parcel of my work.

Despite this, I enjoyed working there. It was far more interesting than what I did before. I was a teenager, I had no plans, no worries, no idea what I was going to do from week to week. My love of football was just about the only constant in my life.

In the 1969/70 season, we went top of the table. Could we maintain it? A 2-1 defeat at Leeds was a setback. However,

Everton would lose only one more league game all season and that was in January at The Dell against Southampton.

The month of March proved pivotal, with six wins out of six. Leeds were hanging on to our coat tails but Catterick had created a winning mentality. One win was all we needed when our bogey team West Brom arrived at Goodison Park.

During this era, many people remember the importance of Harvey, Kendall and Ball, but that does a disservice to the rest of the team. Those three were imperious but they didn't do it all by themselves.

The defence was rock solid. You can't go unbeaten for that long if it isn't. Behind them was goalkeeper Gordon West. He was not only an excellent keeper, he was also one of the game's best characters. There was captain Brian Labone, and players like Joe Royle, Johnny Morrisey, Jimmy Husband and John Hurst.

"Labby" joked afterwards: "We must be the only team to win the league with three players!"

Alan Whittle scored some really important goals towards the end of the season. He was at it again against the Baggies when he found the net after twenty minutes. It didn't just settle the nerves, it sent everyone crazy with excitement.

It was fitting though that the second and decisive goal came from Colin Harvey. It was one worthy of the occasion. I was standing there on the terrace and the moment the ball left Colin's boot, I felt sure it was going in.

When the final whistle went, we all ran onto the pitch.

In 1963, I was a little too young. Seven years later, I was an adult and I was going to make sure that I celebrated this title in style. As the players enjoyed the moment, I didn't know that this would be the last time for fifteen years.

That summer saw the World Cup in Mexico, with England defending the trophy. I'd hoped that manager Sir Alf Ramsey would include Kendall and Harvey in the team to play with Alan Ball.

I'm not just saying that through blue-tinted glasses.

They were the ultimate midfield unit.

Their group game defeat to Brazil is still talked about today, thanks to the incredible save from Gordon Banks. How did he stop that downward header from Pelé? There was the perfect tackle from Bobby Moore too, also thwarting Pelé.

In the quarter- final against West Germany, Ramsey took off Bobby Charlton with England 2-0 ahead. Charlton's absence allowed Franz Beckenbauer more freedom and he used it to his advantage. After pulling it back to 2-2, West Germany won in extra time.

England were going home. Unfortunately, we're still waiting for them to "come home".

1970 wasn't just a big year for football. It was the year when my career totally changed direction.

While working at the hospital, I saw a copy of the Liverpool Weekly News. I'd never heard of it. So I bought a copy and started to read it on my break.

I couldn't believe how much sport was in it. There must have been eight pages, including all the football results from the amateur leagues on Merseyside. At the time, the Liverpool and District Sunday League was the biggest anywhere in Europe.

I enjoyed portering, which gave me lessons in life and about death too. But I began thinking that writing about football could be my vocation.

So I wrote to Ron Carrington, who was the managing director of the paper. I told him I was interested in a career in journalism. Five days after posting the letter, I was at the newspaper office for an interview.

I must have impressed him because a couple of days later, I was offered a job. I wasn't on a contract at Broadgreen Hospital, I had no notice period. I could start the following week. It felt like this was my destiny.

I was about to take the first steps on my journey covering football. Beginning at the Liverpool Weekly News, at the start of the 1970s.

2

The Shakespeare Club

You often hear that if you do a job that you love, then you never have to work a day in your life. At the end of my teens and into my early twenties, I was doing just that.

Imagine being that age and getting paid to watch football and write about it. It didn't matter which team I was covering, I loved my new career path.

No more watching autopsies in the hospital morgue. I was at the local games, and being paid for it.

I wasn't going to settle either. I wanted more.

A friend of mine, Dave Jones, recommended that we check out this place in Liverpool. A lot of people were talking about it. It was attracting big names and was becoming "the place to be" in the city. The Shakespeare Theatre Club on Fraser Street, known locally as "The Shakey" had top-class cabaret.

We decided to pay a visit to coincide with a special night. Bob Monkhouse was top of the bill. Monkhouse was a household name as a popular comedian and TV presenter. His live show certainly had different material in comparison to his television stuff.

Walking into the place was unforgettable. It wouldn't have looked out of place in Stratford-upon-Avon. I looked around and saw people everywhere. Smartly dressed men with glamourous women on their arms. The place felt enormous. You could quickly feel the atmosphere, it was buzzing.

At that moment, I decided that I wanted to explore. There were three tiers and I had a wander round, soaking up the ambience, taking in the surroundings.

Normally there were two acts on before whoever topped the bill. A female singer and a comedian often warmed up the crowd as they dined, before the stars took to the stage. I went up to the second level, where you had the best view. I looked out over a sea of people. The place was magnificent.

Bob Monkhouse had huge star power. He oozed charisma and class. His show was hilarious. I couldn't have picked a better night to go there.

Although Monkhouse was memorable and highly entertaining, there was something else that had a bigger impact on me; the club itself.

One night was all it took. I wanted in. I had to be a part of the place. I just needed to find my opportunity. I wasn't going to leave my day job.

Why would I?

I was progressing quickly as a journalist and it was so enjoyable. But I knew I had to find a way to become part of The Shakey.

I had an idea, one that would benefit me and the venue. I decided to write a piece on The Shakespeare Club. I genuinely wanted to give them some exposure. I contacted them and arranged to interview manager John Birch. He was never going to say no to the free publicity. This was my chance to impress him too. I could kill two birds with one stone. This was my way to get my foot in the door.

The paper covered the club in a positive light and I hit it off with John. After reassuring him that I could juggle my job at the paper and work for him too, he offered me a position.

I was going to live two different lives now, both of which were exciting. Sure, I would be knackered with hardly any sleep, but I didn't care.

I can honestly say that I underestimated how wonderful my time at the club would be.

I felt important, wearing a dinner jacket and bow tie every night for work. My job was to mingle with the revellers and make sure they were happy. I struck up a connection with them. So many of them were regulars and they liked to be looked after. They were spending a fortune; we had to keep hold of customers like that.

I became close with members of Liverpool's underworld. The least said about that, the better!

My links to the club also helped the paper. In the summer of 1972, there was no better example of that.

Roy Orbison was booked to appear for a few days, closing out the show every night. His career had slowed down a bit since the 1960s, but he was still a massive name. I was able to interview him for the paper and spend time with "The Big O" before and after his shows.

This was just another advantage of my job at The Shakey. Orbison had such a presence and was so friendly. There was no ego. He loved performing and chatting with everyone who worked at the club.

Another perfect example of this was Levi Stubbs. The Motown singer was touring with his version of The Four Tops. He'd enjoyed huge success as part of the original group. Now he was doing the rounds with a new edition of the Tops, playing all the hits.

The Shakey booked them to perform one New Year's Eve and they were superb. They went down a storm.

After they'd finished and all the customers had gone, Stubbs asked what we were doing next. It was New Year's Eve after all. We'd planned to have a staff party but nothing major. Stubbs not only wanted to be part of it, he offered to perform for us.

For free.

One person who made an enormous impression on me was Olivia Newton John. She was already a star, but this was years before Grease made her an international celebrity.

Being a true professional, even in the early years of her career, she arrived a day early. She'd been through a tough time. Her name had been dragged through the press because she'd broken up with her fiancé Bruce Welch. He took it very badly. He was part of the band The Shadows, so it was a big story at the time.

Besides taking care of the customers, I was also used to looking after the performers. I went to see how Olivia was doing.

I knocked on her dressing room door and she asked me to come in. As I entered, stood in front of me was one of the most beautiful women I've ever seen.

She was ironing her dress, ready for the next day's show. I introduced myself and told her that she should ask me if she needed anything. I was shocked when she told me that she was alone and had nobody there to help her.

Seeing an opportunity to spend more time with this gorgeous lady, I asked her what she had planned for that evening. She accepted my dinner invitation and we shared a lovely evening together at the restaurant in The Atlantic Hotel, where she was staying.

Olivia was charming, modest and humble. There was an innocence about her, but she also had an aura at the same time.

Everyone enjoyed her show. The locals took Olivia to their hearts and made a real fuss of her when she was spotted walking round the streets of Liverpool. She lapped it up and spent time talking to people. No ego, just a lovely person.

During her short stay in the city, we spent as much of our spare time together as we could. Local hairdresser Herbert Howe pampered her, and club host Pete Price would chaperone her during the day. Olivia was in safe hands with both of them, she wasn't their "type".

Herbert was a larger-than-life character and everyone wanted to go to his salons. If Herbert did your hair for you, you paid top whack too. Sadly, Herbert died far too young.

It was a real pleasure to know Olivia Newton John and I was delighted for her when her career skyrocketed later on. Olivia was one of the nicest celebrities that I've ever spent time with. I was truly saddened by her death.

One day I was asked to look after this baby-faced local comedian. He looked about fifteen but he wasn't that much younger than me. He was just starting out on the ladder and had been doing the rounds in the local clubs.

The Shakey was a great place to get more recognition. But if you failed, word would get round. He did his routine, including a few standard impressions. The audience appreciated him and he went down well.

His name? Les Dennis.

Long before he appeared on TV as part of Russ Abbot's Madhouse and then as a gameshow host, Les was doing the local circuit to get a big break. I asked him after his performance if he wanted to hang around for a bit and have a drink. He couldn't. He had to study the next day!

Les started to get more and more work, his reputation was growing. I was delighted for him, he was such a good lad. Our friendship developed too, and when he married his first wife Lynne, I went to the wedding.

The Shakey didn't just invite established stars. It also helped fresh new talent by giving them a platform to perform.

When Pete Price was on holiday, I stood in for him. That meant I was the club's compere in his absence. I had to address the public and introduce the acts.

That's probably where I built my confidence and ability to improvise in front of a live audience. Both traits would stand me in good stead later in life.

Another female singer who was extremely popular at The Shakey was Sandie Shaw. In the 1960s, she topped the charts three times and also won the Eurovision Song Contest in 1967.

As well as being famous for her singing, Sandie was well-known for performing in bare feet. That might have been fine in a TV studio but in a Liverpool club in the early 1970s, it wasn't recommended!

Every night before she arrived on stage, I took a brush and swept the stage clean. It was just a gag. There I was, in my best suit, brushing the stage in front of a packed house. The crowd thought it was hilarious. Needless to say, I got heckled. I was the best dressed cleaner in the city though!

Off stage, Sandie was great fun. Like many other well-known faces that I met at The Shakey, she was so personable. We shared a love for folk music and both of us took in some of the local clubs so we could enjoy the acts.

One of the most enigmatic people I've ever met was during my time at the club. Irish comedian Dave Allen was brilliant and his repertoire had people in stitches. He'd already been on the BBC for a while and he was enormously successful.

There were two different sides to him. When he wasn't doing his routine for the people, he was very private and didn't mix with anyone.

Before starting his act, he'd relax by reading some seriously heavy literature. Dave Allen was clearly an intelligent man.

When it was time to go on, he put his book down and turned into another persona. He had the audience just where he wanted them and they lapped him up. Then once he'd finished, he returned to his book and continued where he left off.

Allen wasn't rude or impolite, I think he just wanted to be left alone. It was rare for an artist to be like that, but he was a comedy genius. The punters loved him and that was all that mattered.

Nobody got to know him at all during his week at The Shakey.

Another memorable act was Tommy Cooper. Although people thought he was a bit of a clown with his "just like that" catchphrase and his trademark Fez hat, he was an excellent magician. As part of the Magic Circle, he knew how to do a great number of tricks. He was a very funny man.

After he'd put on a great show and the club closed its doors for the night, Tommy made it clear that he wanted to enjoy a drink or two to wind down. I was asked to accompany him. I didn't sit down with him until 2am and he welcomed me warmly to table five. The table we reserved only for VIPs.

"At last, a drinking partner! Let's get some red wine ordered!"

As each glass went down, he started to show off some of his card tricks, with Pete Price joining us. He was getting more and more pissed, but he always had one more trick to perform. It was now 4am and he was still at it. I felt terrible, the red wine was not agreeing with me but Tommy was on form. I didn't think he was ever going to stop.

Finally, the red wine got the better of him and we called it a night. I never touch red wine but it always reminds me of Tommy Cooper, sat at table five in The Shakey, asking me "Is this your card?"

Combining my two jobs was hard work. I was exhausted. But adrenaline got me through it – along with the odd sneaky nap here and there.

It was worth it.

The newspaper helped me get on the ladder in media. Working at The Shakey made me feel ten feet tall. For a bloke who's five foot six, that was a great feeling!

Being around interesting people, mixing with the city's rich and looking after the acts was some experience.

But it was as part of my day job that I first met one of Liverpool's biggest ever legends.

And it didn't get off to a good start.

3

Meeting Mr Shankly

When Ken Rogers, a colleague at the paper, moved to the Liverpool Echo, I stepped into his shoes. I was now the Sports Editor!

That sounds impressive doesn't it? It was nowhere near as big or important as it sounds. I had nobody under me. I was the Sports Editor of a one-man team – me. However, I had the freedom to manage the content. I thought it was time for me to make my mark.

Instead, I opened Pandora's Box.

I decided to link Clyde Best of West Ham to Liverpool, as he was having a purple patch. I made a big deal out of it. Nobody else had the story anywhere. This would be a massive scoop for us.

The day the paper came out, that story was the main one in the sports pullout.

It was total fiction.

I was sat reading it when my colleague Pat Gaskell told me that someone was on the phone claiming to be Bill Shankly. I laughed and scoffed. I didn't believe it but said I'd take the call anyway.

It had to be a wind up. Bill Shankly didn't read our paper, did he?

I answered and the person on the other end of the line was straight to the point.

"Hullo? Bill Shankly here."

He paused. A split second felt like an hour as I tried to work out if it was really him.

"Yer the fella that wrote that FUCKIN' story aboot Clyde Best?"

I started to sweat. It really was Bill Shankly. His Scottish accent and intonation were instantly recognisable. All my cockiness drained out of me.

I was shitting myself.

This was the most respected and feared football manager in the country on the phone. The man was adored in Liverpool and practically walked on water.

And he was pissed off.

Pissed off with the newspaper.

But worse than that. He was furious with me!

I nervously muttered my reply, confessing to him that I indeed wrote the piece. I gulped as I waited for his response. I feared the biggest bollocking of my life coming. To say he was unhappy about the situation is putting it mildly.

"Where the fuck did ye get that frum? We have nae interest whatsoever in Clyde Best. Why didnae ye ring me, before ye put it in print?"

He was raging.

I apologised and told him that I got the information from a source. Of course there was no source. I invented the whole thing. It was total bullshit.

Bill Shankly hadn't finished with me yet. He knew I was lying.

"Ye a newspaper man, ye should have good sources, not people makin' things up."

I was blushing and frightened to death. His lecture was justified and I felt like a little kid. I was just glad it was by phone and not face to face.

"Ye need tae understand son. Ye need tae understand how football works."

I humbly told him that I'd appreciate any advice he could give me. Without changing his tone, he told me to come to his office at Anfield the following week.

When I arrived at the ground, he greeted me with his hands on his hips, his eyes staring at me. He was wearing what I consider to be his trademark look. A shirt, red tie and a mac. He made sure his posture was perfect.

Was he trying to intimidate me?

He didn't have to try very hard! I later realised that this was Bill's way. He was just showing me who was boss.

We went to the Liverpool training ground at Melwood, where I observed the players first hand. Afterwards, we went back to his office, so I could see the master at work.

The ice had been broken and the Clyde Best story was now in the past. I was able to turn this experience into a full-page article "A Day in the Life of a Football Manager – Bill Shankly".

When the paper came out with the feature in, I called Bill at Anfield to see if he'd read it. The formalities of calling him Mr Shankly had been dismissed during my visit to the club. Indeed he had. His answer was not only a huge relief but gave me my confidence back.

"Ye got it right son. Ye got it dead right."

What started as a terrifying introduction to Bill Shankly had gone full circle. He was now praising me. Not only that, a bond was forming between us.

Don't forget I was young and naïve. I thought I was the bee's knees, but I wasn't. I probably needed bringing down a peg or two. Perhaps my role at The Shakey had made me a bit too overconfident.

I couldn't think of a better person to teach me a lesson than Bill Shankly. He opened the doors to his inner sanctum for me. Bill wanted me to witness how the club was run. He didn't have to do that. I imagine Shanks knew that I wouldn't disappoint him a second time. I was too afraid to let him down again.

My first ever dealings with Bill Shankly finished with a positive conclusion. There would be many more memorable experiences with the great man, as we grew closer later on.

I might have had the red carpet rolled out for me by Bill Shankly but there was another club in the area that welcomed me with open arms too. This one wasn't quite as famous but I had great fun covering them.

South Liverpool were in the Northern Premier League at a time when there was some real quality to be found outside of the Football League.

A perfect example was John Aldridge, who made it to the big time after starting at South Liverpool. A local lad, John went to Newport County and then Oxford United before landing his dream move to Anfield. A prolific scorer wherever he went, Aldridge won many caps for Ireland too.

There was another star who came through the South Liverpool ranks a fair few years before Aldridge; Jimmy Case.

South Liverpool's manager Alan Hampson was on holiday, so he asked me to go to a Sunday league cup final. He wanted me to keep an eye on this young prospect. It was Jimmy. He must have only been about sixteen.

I always joke that I discovered Jimmy, which is absolutely false but I certainly knew of him before most people.

I've done some events with Jimmy and we've been mates for years. I use that story as an anecdote. Casey, being a good sport, plays along and tells everyone that I was the one who unearthed him.

As I said, it's not strictly true, but it's a good tale to tell.

I was always trying to do something different, especially where South Liverpool FC was concerned. I used to train with them and travel to away games on the team bus.

I loved non-league football. Watching South was similar to watching Macclesfield. The paper sold very well in the south end of the city, particularly in Garston where Holly Park, South's ground, was situated.

Alan "Hampy" Hampson and I got on really well. On one occasion we were travelling north for a fixture, when a player fell ill. If the truth be known, he was pissed. That left South Liverpool with just eleven men.

Hampy's solution was simple; he stuck me on the bench. I was shitting myself in case a player got injured and I had to go on. Thankfully, I remained an "unused" sub.

Another time, we were back on my old stomping ground; Macclesfield. This time it was the trainer's turn to be ill (he wasn't pissed) so I was in charge of the bucket and sponge. I became the trainer for that match.

During the game, right back Arthur Goldstein was on the wrong end of a bad tackle. He went down in some discomfort. I was watching on, sat next to Hampy, who turned and looked at me.

"Go on, sort him out!"

"What?"

"You're the trainer, go on!"

So I legged it onto the field, armed with the bucket and sponge.

"Where's it hurt Arth?"

"Me knee, it's killing me."

I took the sponge, which was soaking with cold water, and started putting it on his knee.

"What the fuck are you doing??"

"I don't fucking know!"

Afterwards, the lads were laughing about it all the way back to Garston.

Did you know that in September 1949, South Liverpool made history?

They hosted the very first game in England under permanent floodlights. It was a friendly against a Nigerian XI.

As little-known facts go, that takes some beating.

I had a free reign at the Weekly News. I edited my own copy and laid out the sports pages for publication.

By the end of my four years at the paper, I was made group sports editor which meant editing the Widnes and Runcorn papers as well. The Liverpool paper's editor Keith Charlton and the group's managing editor, Ron Carrington, put a lot of trust in me.

So let me take you back to a Tuesday night game under the lights with South in action against Great Harwood. I wanted to do something special for Thursday's edition.

On a whim I went to Bellefield, Everton's training ground, and introduced myself to Colin Harvey to ask him if he'd be guest reporter for the game.

Colin didn't hesitate.

"Sounds like fun," said one of my absolute heroes.

"There's no money in it, Colin."

That didn't deter him, so we arranged to meet on the Tuesday evening. Colin and I sat together in the stand at Holly Park. Colin was doing a running commentary with me taking notes in shorthand.

Colin's reading of the game was illuminating. I almost hate to say so, but it was probably the best match report I'd ever written.

Under the headline, in big bold letters it said:

by Colin Harvey

I was dead chuffed and so were Messrs Charlton and Carrington.

I made a lot of friends during my time covering South Liverpool. One might surprise you.

Stan Boardman's best mate, Colin Bridge, was South's left back. Stan was a regular at Holly Park before he began doing the comedy circuit. Between them, Bridgie and Stan were like a comedy double act.

Great company.

Some nights they'd turn up at The Shakey and I'd get them in for "nowt". Colin passed away far too early, but Stan and I remain good pals. We live about 10 minutes apart and often meet up for a coffee in Heswall.

Two old "fockers" chewing the fat.

It was also at the paper where the name Elton Welsby began. Prior to that, I was known as Roger E. Welsby.

Yes, Roger.

A colleague, Ken Welsby (no relation) asked me what the E stood for. After that Elt became a nickname and it stuck.

I thoroughly enjoyed my time at the paper. It was a good grounding. I paid a visit to their HQ in Widnes, in the late 1980s. At the time they were editing the Widnes and Runcorn papers for the following day. They appeared somewhat under the cosh when I breezed in.

"Need a hand?"

It was back into the old routine for a fun-filled afternoon, which was hugely enjoyable. Then it was off to a nearby social club for snooker and a few beers. Even "Big C" (Carrington) came for a drink.

That was pretty rare.

Right, back to the 1970s.

In May 1974, Liverpool comfortably beat Newcastle United 3-0 in the FA Cup final. It turned out to be Bill Shankly's final game in charge of the club. He was 60 years old.

In his own book, he said that in the dressing room after the cup final, he knew it was time. Bill had given everything to build Liverpool. They were in the Second Division when he took over. Not only did he turn them into champions, he laid the foundations for the future.

Many years later I was talking to Peter Robinson, who'd been Liverpool's club secretary and involved at Anfield for decades. It's no exaggeration to say that, in my opinion, Peter Robinson was the finest administrator in football. There's been nobody better.

Peter told me that not long after Shanks made his decision to retire, Bill had second thoughts. It was too late. Bob Paisley had already been named as his successor.

Bill still wanted to be around the club though. He'd turn up and watch training at Melwood. Liverpool had taken over his life, and entirely walking away was not an option for him.

The club was in a difficult position. Bill was a legend, but they also needed to give Bob space to do his job.

The players were uncomfortable. Their old boss was there but they needed to listen to and work with the new one. Bob felt that Bill was undermining his authority. His former players were still calling him boss. But Bob Paisley was now in charge. Shanks was told to stop going.

Over at Everton, Bill had an open invitation. It's incredible to think about. The former manager of our biggest rivals, who'd competed against us and made Liverpool into this great side, was welcome to visit Everton.

Shanks lived right opposite the Everton training ground. He could see the whole place out of one of his windows. Tommy Docherty at Manchester United made it clear that Bill could come to Old Trafford whenever he wanted to.

That's how much Liverpool's two biggest rivals respected Bill.

Now in retirement, what would a man like Shanks do to pass his time?

I'd find out soon enough.

Bill Shankly wasn't the only one who felt like he needed a change.

I'd done as much as I could with the paper. It'd been a great experience but I was itching for more. I was confident in my own abilities now and working at The Shakey meant that I was starting to become known around the city.

Spending time with so many stars also made me realise that I was comfortable around them. I craved something else. Something more challenging than a local newspaper.

The city of Liverpool was about to get a new radio station. I was intrigued and thought that this could be the next step for me. The date was set for Radio City to launch. 21st October 1974. I wanted to be part of it. I had a lot of good contacts on Merseyside.

There was a real buzz about Radio City. Liverpool is famous for its music, and the people were relishing the thought of something new. It felt like the perfect opportunity for me to take the next step on the career ladder.

Something bigger was on the horizon, and it was certainly a case of being in the right place at the right time again.

4

Radio City

As the last days of summer turned to autumn in 1974, the city of Liverpool was preparing for its new radio station.

It had got people talking. They wanted something vibrant and dynamic. Something that they could relate to. Nobody knew what to expect, but they were excited to find out.

The thought of being a part of Radio City appealed to me. I'd been doing some occasional work for BBC Radio Merseyside, reading out the football and racing results. This new station had so much going for it. I just needed an opportunity.

Looking back on the 1970s, a lot of what happened to me professionally came down to timing.

I was at Radio Merseyside one day minding my own business. In the same room was Eddie Hemmings, who later became famous for his work in rugby league. He was on the phone to David Maker of Radio City.

Eddie had been offered a job at the new station, but after thinking about it, he decided to stay with the BBC. I heard every word of the conversation. I was sat right there.

I instinctively left the room and ran to the phone box on the street outside of Radio Merseyside. I had to get my breath back first before calling David Maker. I got through to him, explained who I was and told him about my experience at the newspaper and Radio Merseyside. I asked him outright if he had anything at Radio City for me. I had nothing to lose.

After being turned down by Eddie, Maker was panicking. The launch date was approaching and he needed someone to work alongside new sports editor Wally Scott.

Wally was a respected journalist in Liverpool and was a huge part of Mercury Press. That company was owned by Terry Smith, who was also the founder and managing director of Radio City.

Wally was a great choice to bring in to work at the station. David Maker was sure that Eddie would take the job and work with Wally. David had no plan B when Eddie said no.

The clock was ticking, there was just over a week before the station was due to go on air. With his back against the wall, he asked me to come down and see him. I told him that I could be there in ten minutes and like that I set off.

Less than an hour after overhearing David's conversation with Eddie, he offered me a job. He wanted me to start straight away. This was the chance I wanted, I wasn't going to turn it down.

David took me around the building, which wasn't even finished yet. He wanted me to learn the technology and understand how everything worked. I had about a week to grasp it all. It was impossible.

I was so grateful to work with Wally Scott though. He became a true mentor for me. Wally's help and advice over my four-year spell at the station was invaluable.

On 21st October 1974, Radio City went live and so did I. During the news, I did the sports bulletin. It was nerve-wracking. I was out of the comfort zone of the newspaper now.

I'll be the first to admit that I've never been great with technology. Now I was learning on the job with a live audience listening in.

The very first week we had an experience that was like something out of a slapstick comedy. We had a midweek sports programme, with Wally presenting. I have no idea how it happened, but the tape went spiralling into the air.

Wally had to improvise, while at the same time an engineer was frantically trying to put things right. It was a real mess and we felt like amateurs. It would've been hilarious to watch the scene unfold.

I wasn't a big name for the new station to have on air, but very quickly they brought in someone who would give the ratings a spike. He might have retired from management but Bill Shankly wasn't going to go away quietly.

Radio City offered him his own chat show. His first guest was none other than the Prime Minister Harold Wilson.

Naturally, the majority of the country would be nervous when sat in front of the Prime Minister. But this was Bill Shankly. He wasn't fazed by anyone. He respected Harold Wilson, but Bill's personality was strong enough to interview him. And of course he did it in true Shankly style.

Wally and I were there, behind the glass watching this meeting of minds.

The most powerful man in Britain. And Harold Wilson!

Bill began by addressing Wilson by his official title but quickly the Prime Minister asked him to call him by his first name. The two of them together were just magic.

Bill being Bill asked Wilson a remarkable question:

"Harold, d'ye know who the first socialist was?"

Wilson took a puff of his pipe, while he pondered for a moment.

"Who's that Bill? Was it Ramsay MacDonald?" replied the Prime Minister.

Bill's answer was classic Shankly.

"Na. It was Jesus Christ."

It was hard for us to contain ourselves. Bill had pulled out another classic.

Wilson's reaction was priceless. His mouth dropped open. He didn't see that one coming. However, not long after, we could only hear both of them. Wilson was smoking his pipe so much the studio turned misty. This was the 1970s; it was completely normal to smoke at work.

After the interview, Wilson departed with his security team. We were so happy with how it went. However, Shanks made a beeline for me. I can remember it like it was yesterday. I was thinking "What's up with him?"

Bill wasn't happy. He marched over and then stopped in front of me. Shanks looked straight into my eyes.

"Elton son, he tried tae steal ma fuckin' thunder."

Shanks had a big ego and he'd come up against someone who was also used to being the centre of attention. The two of them were fighting for the last word.

Either myself or Wally would toss a coin to see who picked Shanks up from home to bring him into the studio to record his programme. If I called heads, I wanted it to be tails so it was down to Wally.

You never knew what you were going to get from Bill. He was so unpredictable. Often Wally would drop Shanks off and then whisper to me, "He's on one today Elt!"

One Saturday, Wally felt Bill was in a particularly grumpy mood. To counter it, Wally had a card up his sleeve. He enquired how Bill's grandkids were doing. Shanks adored his grandchildren, so it seemed like a safe bet.

Wally joined me afterwards, shaking his head.

"Well Elt, I asked about his grandkids, even that didn't work."

Bill snapped: "Fuckin' little gits, Wally, they're eatin' me oot of hoose an' home."

Sometimes you couldn't win.

The Bill Shankly show with Harold Wilson was a huge success, so other guests were booked. One proved to be particularly memorable. The singer Lulu. However, Shanks didn't really know much about her.

Shanks had heard of Lulu and knew what she did. But that was all. Bill loved three other Scottish singers; Kenneth McKellar, Andy Stewart and Moira Anderson.

We contemplated getting one of them to come on the show, but a Merseyside audience was never going to relate to an interview like that. Lulu was well-known throughout the country.

The interview began with Bill introducing her and she warmly greeted her fellow Scot. Except she did so with an English accent. She began talking about the start of her career in Scotland but sounded like she was a character in Eastenders.

Bill raised his eyebrows. He wasn't amused. He had to address this. I'd seen that look in his eyes before. I knew what was coming.

Shankly stared at her and then began to speak. His voice was hard and his Scottishness seemed to be accentuated. His tone was slow and purposeful.

"Excuse me, lassie, yer tellin' me, yer tellin' me that yer frum Glasgow?" asked Bill.

Lulu replied that was indeed the case. She was still speaking like a Cockney.

Bill couldn't let this go.

"D'ye think that great Scottish warriors like Robert the Bruce and William Wallace would go tae London and start speakin' like that?"

Bill didn't let up.

"A'm startin' tae ascertain, yer name, isnae really…Lulu."

She changed characters and Lulu was gone.

"Nae, it's Marie, Marie Lawrie."

She replied in broad Scottish.

"Well, A'm talkin' tae Marie," said Bill.

We had a problem.

Thankfully the interviews were recorded on Saturday mornings and then played later in the afternoon for the fans going to the matches to listen to. For the second part, I had to do a voiceover that went something like this:

"Welcome to part two of the Bill Shankly Show with his guest Lulu. Now you might be confused because Lulu doesn't sound anything like Lulu. Bill isn't calling her Lulu. But take my word for it, it really is Lulu. Now back to the show."

If I hadn't have done it, anyone tuning in halfway through would never have known who Bill was talking to. They wouldn't have had a clue. Some stars would never have put up with this type of behaviour or line of questioning. But not everyone was interviewed by Bill Shankly.

We went back to Shanks.

"Welcome back! A'm talkin' wi Marie."

Working for Radio City wasn't only elevating my career, but it was giving me more opportunities to spend time with Bill. Our bond had already been formed following the Clyde Best incident. Now we were colleagues.

Despite his demeanour and reputation, Shanks was a lovely man. And we were going to be in each other's company a lot more.

Before the FA Cup 3rd round in 1975, I had to go to Bill's home to record an interview with him about the matches from that weekend. He was so welcoming, as his wife Nessie brought cup after cup of tea and plates of biscuits.

At the end of the interview, I asked him which cup tie would cause a surprise. A smile came to his face and he leant forward.

"The only thing that surprises me aboot the cup, is that people are surprised."

Nessie came with more tea. And Bill repeated the line again.

And again.

I had to get back to the studio, but he wanted to carry on chatting.

The following year, Bob Paisley won the Manager of the Year Award and Bill was asked to present it to him. Shanks had no problem with this and gladly accepted the invitation. In my capacity at the radio station, I was to cover the ceremony in London.

Bill asked me if I was going and when I told him that I was, he recommended that we travel together.

"We'll take the train an' drink tea, a' the way there," he insisted.

That's exactly what we did. I'm sure we had a fresh pot every quarter of an hour. From Liverpool to London, just me and Bill Shankly drinking tea. You couldn't put a price on an experience like that. And there was more to come.

When it was time for Bob Paisley to receive the award, Bill took to the stage and addressed the audience. He began speaking in a calm manner.

"Ye might be thinkin' that A'm jealous, daein' this for Bob."

Then he raised his voice to finish his sentence.

"Well, yer FUCKIN' right!"

The audience was stunned. This was the mid-1970s and it was rare to hear people swear in public like that. Plus, this was Bill Shankly.

Perhaps he'd drunk too much tea!

There was a split-second delay, before everyone burst into laughter. Then they broke out into rounds of applause. He got away with it. He was Bill Shankly.

While writing this book, Wally Scott died. The news hit me hard.

Without Wally's help, there's no way I would've got as far as I did. I wanted to say thanks to him in print and for him to read the book. It was a brilliant time and I would've loved Wally to have been able to reminisce about those days.

So here's a classic Wally Scott story for you. Wally eventually teamed up as a comedian with his co-host, Billy Butler, presenting a show on Radio Merseyside called "Hold Your Plums".

It became the most iconic show with an astonishing number of listeners every Sunday. Basically, it was where scousers phoned in on a variety of subjects including a very tongue-in-cheek quiz.

For those of you who have no idea of the show, here are a couple of snippets.

"Okay, the next question is...

...what was Hitler's first name?"

Phone rings.

"Hello love, have you got the answer?"

"Hitler's first name was..."

Pause...

"Was it Heil, Bill?"

Wally falls about laughing.

Now I can tell you that Bob Paisley was a massive fan of the show. He thought it just epitomised scouse humour.

Now it was Wally's turn to ask a question.

"Name the Hollywood actor who starred in countless Westerns.

First name, Gary."

Listener: "Gizza clue, Wally."

"His second name is also the name of a car."

"Ermm...you got me there Wal."

"Have a guess."

"Was it Gary Datsun?"

It was non-stop and Wally was brilliant. If you'd have told me on the night he was struggling to ad-lib his way through our first sports programme on Radio City, that he'd end up being one of the funniest guys on local radio, I'd have had you committed.

Thank you, Wally Scott, for everything you did for me and for being such an important part of my life.

Rest in peace my friend. I'll never forget you.

5

Taking the Mic

For an Evertonian, covering sport for the local radio station would seem like a dream job. Except I didn't get the chance to cover many of their games. Also, because I was working, I wasn't able to watch them play as much as I'd have liked either.

Terry Smith was an enormous Liverpool fan, as was Wally. Terry was more blinkered than Wally though, it was like Everton didn't exist to him. Wally would give us credit. He wasn't as biased as Terry.

The 1970s was a frustrating time for Everton. Winning the title in 1970 meant that we peaked within the first five months of the decade!

When the radio station launched in October 1974, the football season had already begun. Everton were doing well under manager Billy Bingham. It was far from the best side I'd ever seen in blue, but they were a real team.

I was doing the Everton versus Altrincham FA Cup tie in early 1975 at Goodison Park. Every Saturday afternoon, London Weekend Television (LWT) broadcast World of Sport all over the country. It was a mix of different sports.

The programme became famous for showing British wrestling too. Think Big Daddy versus Giant Haystacks in a smoky hall with old ladies waving their handbags at the grapplers.

Hosted by the legendary Dickie Davies, World of Sport would update everyone on the football scores before offering a full results service. You'll hear more about that later.

In 1975, it started a new format, which involved going to the local reporters at the different games so they could explain what was happening. I wasn't going to interact directly with Dickie, I would just briefly go over the latest information.

When the non-league side took a shock lead, I became the first to ever use this new method of reporting.

Dickie introduced me and off I went.

Except the person at the studio in London said it hadn't worked. The technology was new and they hadn't got to grips with it yet. So I did a second take. Then a third. I was told there was still a problem, so I did it for a fourth time.

It was amateur hour at LWT and it was getting ridiculous. Then they told me that in fact my first attempt had gone live and that everything was fine. I don't know what they were playing at, but it was a farce.

Thankfully, they got over these teething troubles. This style of reporting became commonplace. Today, when we watch the different football programmes on a Saturday afternoon on the BBC or Sky Sports, we see the presenter go around the grounds all the time.

I was the guinea pig for this back in 1975.

In the title race, Everton were top in late March. They had to play away to rock-bottom Carlisle United while second placed Liverpool were at home to Birmingham City. A solitary point separated the two Merseyside clubs.

Terry told me that I'd be working at Anfield but I asked to go to Carlisle instead. He wouldn't have it. I pushed and pushed and he finally gave in.

I headed further north to commentate on the match. It was a terrible day for Evertonians. Carlisle won 3-0, and after Liverpool beat Birmingham, there were new leaders. The season petered out and Everton came fourth.

That summer I joined in Everton's pre-season training. It was easy to understand why the team had been sharp for most of the season. The training was so physically difficult.

Billy had them working hard. They were on the sand dunes at Southport.

Billy had made a course for us to run around. I managed to keep up with Bob Latchford and I ran alongside him. Latch had arrived from Birmingham City and had become a massive hero at Goodison Park thanks to his goalscoring exploits. Bob and I gave it our best but we reached a point where we couldn't carry on. We collapsed in a heap on the floor.

We were both out of breath and panting like two tired old dogs. Latch looked back and saw Mick Lyons catching us up.

"Elt, we can't be doing that bad if Lyonsie's behind us."

"He's fucking lapping us, Latch!!" I replied with sweat pouring down my face.

Then I threw up.

In my eyes, Mick Lyons was Mr Everton during this period. He was a phenomenal servant to the club. Billy Bingham put a picture on the wall of the dressing room to show everyone the type of spirit he wanted.

The photo was of Mick bravely scoring a header against Leeds, surrounded by some of the hardest players in the game like Norman Hunter. Boots were flying but Mick put his head in where it hurts. To Billy, this was the epitome of what was needed to play for Everton. Mick Lyons was the example that everyone needed to follow.

Despite the gruelling training sessions, Everton looked to be going backwards after their near-miss in 1975. By the end of 1976, the pressure was too much and Billy Bingham left the club. A run of five defeats in eight games was considered to be unacceptable. The rot had sent in.

It was another taxi ride, courtesy of Sir John Moores.

I felt bad for Billy, he'd done his best and I liked him. I often wonder what might have been if we could have got over the finishing line the previous year. Now Billy was gone and a replacement was quickly in place.

Gordon Lee became the new boss in January 1977. Gordon was very different to Billy and had been growing his reputation at Newcastle United. He didn't get off to a good start on or off the field. The defeats continued, but it was at his first meeting with the press that he put himself in a difficult spot.

Asked by a journalist which players he'd like to sign, Gordon's reply turned heads. He started off with Ray Clemence. He then continued. He listed the whole Liverpool team. An Everton manager could never admit this in public. Even though Liverpool were the best.

This was 1977 so it was behind closed doors. With no social media or 24-hour news coverage, his comments stayed in the room. The media protected him that day. It was the way things were done back then.

At a later press conference, Gordon announced that a young lad was making his debut at right back.

"What's his name Gordon?"

"Borrows."

"What's his first name?"

"Dunno…but the lads call him Bugsy."

Gordon was unpredictable and far from worldly wise. He'd sometimes go off on a tangent. I was interviewing him after a home game against Wolves. A thriller. But he seemed a bit grumpy. We talked about the game but he obviously had something else on his mind.

"You seem a bit distracted, Gordon?"

"Yes, one team let me down on my accumulator... Stenfuckinhousebastardmuir."

The Scottish team Stenhousemuir had lost, so Gordon's bet was up the spout.

We'd been "live".

Gordon had no filter. He'd use bad language without thinking. It was part of his everyday vocabulary. My wife Joyce and I were invited to Jimmy McGregor's house for dinner one night. Stevie Coppell and his wife Jane were also invited. As Jimmy was Everton's physio at the time, Gordon and his wife were there too.

We had a lovely time but Gordon was dropping the "F bomb" constantly. None of us are prudes. I looked at Steve and he glanced over at Jane. She looked back at me and mouthed:

"Is he always like this?"

I just nodded.

On one particular occasion, I travelled with the Everton lads to an away match. It wasn't the best of games but Duncan McKenzie scored an important goal on a woeful pitch. It was a mud bath.

The ball had got stuck and stayed behind Duncan. He managed to take control of it and then get a shot off. The ball rolled towards the net, then got stuck on the line. Duncan had to run in and finish it off. It was a ridiculous goal but it didn't matter.

It mattered to his manager though.

Gordon wasn't a fan of flair players, and on the way back he made his feelings known about Duncan's finish.

"Bloody McKenzie. Worra ugly goal. Goals like that shouldn't fucking count. Terrible."

It didn't stop there. He went off on one of his tangents.

"When I was at Newcastle, all the bloody fans were singing 'Jimmy, Jimmy Smith, Jinky Jimmy Smith'. So Jinky decides to dribble past one. Then another. A third. They're still singing his fucking name. Then fucking Jinky loses the ball. The other team go up the other end and fucking score. JINKY FUCKIN' SMITH!"

Jimmy Smith was a fan favourite at Newcastle because of his mazy runs and his flair. He was an exciting player. But like Duncan McKenzie, he wasn't a Gordon Lee player.

Gordon managed to steady the ship and after a home defeat to Leicester City on 12th February, Everton lost only two more league games for the rest of the campaign.

The cups were proving a source of excitement for the fans too. Reaching the League Cup final, it took two replays before Aston Villa triumphed 3-2 at Old Trafford.

There was still the FA Cup, with the Blues making it to the semi-final.

Standing in their way? Liverpool.

Over 52,000 made the short journey to Maine Road, home of Manchester City, for the all-Merseyside clash. A place at Wembley was at stake. In my Radio City capacity, I was at Maine Road and what unfolded is still discussed today by Evertonians of a certain vintage.

Liverpool went in front early on through Terry McDermott before Duncan McKenzie levelled for the Blues. Even Gordon Lee must have appreciated that! But in the second half, Jimmy Case made it 2-1.

Time was ticking away. Then Bruce Rioch popped up to tap in at the far post to equalise with just seven minutes left. The pendulum had swung and Everton fancied their chances now.

With moments to go, Ronny Goodlass sent in a cross from the left wing. He found Bryan Hamilton. Hammy got a touch and sent the ball past Clemence. He wheeled away while the Liverpool lads looked shell-shocked.

Then it happened.

Ref Clive Thomas wasn't pointing towards the centre spot but to where Bryan Hamilton had done WHAT??

Handball? Encroached into an offside position. WHAT??

It finished 2-2 and at the final whistle I headed to the dressing room area to wait for the players and Clive Thomas. When Thomas came out of his room I was straight in.

"Mr Thomas, why was Bryan Hamilton's goal disallowed?"

"Offside."

Okay, but what followed was baffling and made me think the little referee was on an ego trip. I followed him up the steps to where the written press was congregated.

Norman Wynn of the People asked him the same question I did.

"Handball."

It was a total contradiction to what he'd said minutes earlier. Eventually the reason given was an infringement.

Bollocks!

He goofed and wouldn't/couldn't admit it. Liverpool won the replay 3-0. The chance had gone. Thomas awarded the Reds an early penalty and we never recovered.

Clive Thomas was no stranger to controversy. Most notably when he disallowed a goal from Brazilian Zico at the 1978 World Cup. He blew his whistle while the ball was still in the air from a corner kick. Ridiculous.

The ironic thing is that despite my affiliation to Everton, through my work on the radio, I became close to many Liverpool players as the Bob Paisley era began and they hoovered up the trophies.

And they treated me like one of their own.

6

Friends not foes

As Everton toiled through the 1970s, Liverpool Football Club got better and better. Bill Shankly leaving in 1974 was huge news but it didn't cause Liverpool any damage at all. Bill had built the club so well that his successor came from within. Bob Paisley took the baton from Shanks.

I had to provide the voice for some of their biggest and best moments. I wanted to be as professional as possible, that's all.

Due to my role, Liverpool welcomed me with open arms. While Everton fans looked at them as rivals, I was friends with their players. I felt like an insider.

When I married my fiancée Joyce in 1976, my best man was Ray Clemence. We did things socially with Clem and his wife Vee. Ian Callaghan and Roy Evans too. One afternoon, Clem, Cally, Roy and I had a game of golf at Formby then met up with the ladies at Clem's house for a BBQ.

Then it started to piss it down.

Like that was going to stop us. One of us, and I can't pinpoint who, thought it would be a good idea to go ahead and do the BBQ in the garage.

What a terrible idea! There was more smoke than when Harold Wilson lit up his pipe!

With Liverpool, there was a mutual trust and respect, despite my allegiance to Everton. And that wasn't a secret either. Bob Paisley turned to me one day and invited me to travel on the team bus. So more often than not, I went on the coach with the players and staff.

I always sat right behind the driver at the front. After the match, the players were at the back unwinding, normally with a crate of beer. Even though I knew them and we were on good terms, I never wanted to bother them. That was their time.

Bob would have a wander up and down the aisle and chat to Ronnie Moran, Roy Evans and Joe Fagan. Just to show you how relaxed Bob Paisley was, he'd be wearing his slippers! Afterwards, when he'd finished with the staff, he came and sat by me. I always gave him a cigar by way of thank you.

My time at Radio City coincided with Liverpool becoming the best in Europe.

They'd already won the UEFA Cup in 1973. In the 1975/76 season, Liverpool embarked on another European adventure after a couple of years of disappointment on the continent.

I was now installed as the lead voice of football on the station, so naturally I was there for all of these games.

They squeezed through past Scottish side Hibernian after losing the first leg in Edinburgh before destroying Real Sociedad. The third round draw paired Liverpool with Śląsk Wrocław.

The trip was unforgettable.

We flew to Warsaw, but it was still a two or three-hour bus ride from the airport to Wrocław. I can't explain how cold it was outside. People were visibly shivering.

A coach was provided for the Liverpool entourage and they travelled in style. It was state of the art for the time.

I was gathered with the rest of the media when another bus arrived. It was prehistoric. We laughed our heads off, pointing at this decrepit old thing. Who was going to get on that?

Then it dawned on us. The bus was for us. The Liverpool lads set off, while were herded onto our bus.

It felt even colder inside than it did outside. We were freezing and there was no heating to warm us up. We couldn't have ruled out getting hyperthermia.

Then came a saviour.

He was the famous photographer, Harry Ormesher. Harry was always booked by Evel Knievel when he came to Britain for one of his spectacular jumps. No matter how Evel landed, whatever state he was in, Harry had to photograph him.

Harry was our hero that day. He produced a bottle of vodka from his bag. A few of the newspaper lads had been to duty free and had stocked up. The vodka bottle was passed around and suddenly we started to warm up.

That bottle didn't last long.

To great cheers, a whisky bottle then appeared and it was again shared amongst us all. This continued, as all the duty-free drinks that they'd purchased were consumed. It was the only form of heating available to us.

After what seemed like an eternity, we arrived in Wrocław. The Liverpool players were waiting for us. They'd just got off their coach. It was so cold that the windows on our coach were frozen. The moment the driver stopped, we headed for the exit. Everyone was desperate to get off that bus.

Phil Neal opened the door for us and we tumbled down like dominoes and onto the road. Each and every one of us was so pissed that we couldn't get off the bus gracefully.

The Liverpool lads were in stitches as we tried to get back to our feet. We were in such a state. We were skidding all over the place and struggling to stand up.

Damn those icy roads!

We were all staying in the same place, a Holiday Inn. The journalists and the Liverpool lads together. I was on the same floor as Tommy Smith. But before I could get settled, I had to ring Radio City and do a live piece.

There was just one problem. I was bladdered.

From a phone box in the foyer, I called through to the studio and I tried my best to sound as normal as possible. It wasn't easy. The more you try to appear sober when you're shitfaced, the harder it is.

I started well, explaining that the Liverpool squad had arrived at the hotel and that I'd be interviewing Bob Paisley later. No problem, everything was going to plan.

Then I came out with the following cracker:

"I confidently predict that Liverpool will win both ties of this leg."

Then it got worse.

Kevin Keegan walked by and saw me on the phone and shouted:

"Hey Elt, put that bird down, you don't know where she's been!"

Kevin had no idea who I was on the phone to. He certainly didn't know that I was live on air. His comment was picked up and heard by the listeners back on Merseyside.

One of them was my future mother-in-law. Without hesitation, she called Joyce.

"Elton's playing bloody games. He's not been in Poland for five minutes and he's already got a bloody bird."

Cheers Kev!

Later that night, there was a huge amount of noise coming from the corridor. It was an attempt from the locals to disturb the Liverpool players so they'd be knackered for the next day. I left my room to see what was happening.

The next minute, Tommy Smith walked out of his room. He wasn't best pleased.

Tommy was a top bloke and a great friend for years. He had his hard nut reputation on the field but he also looked the part off it too. You wouldn't want to get on his wrong side. And when he was annoyed, you didn't want to be in the vicinity. He'd been disturbed by this group of people.

Thankfully he kept his cool, as Ronnie Moran arrived on the scene. The first thing Ronnie saw was a pissed off Tommy Smith, looking over at the noisy locals. As I was stood with the group, Ronnie let me have it.

"What's fucking happening? Is this something to do with you?"

Tommy stepped in. He turned to Ronnie and in no uncertain terms put the record straight.

The locals might not have understood English but when they saw Tommy's body language, they got the message. He stared at them one last time, and they cleared off. Ronnie came to me the next day and apologised.

Liverpool won the first leg 2-1 and a Jimmy Case hat trick finished the job at Anfield. The quarter-final draw then paired them with East German side Dynamo Dresden. After beating them, the big test awaited in the semi-final; Barcelona.

The Spanish side had a ghost from Liverpool's past in their ranks. Johan Cruyff was now a global icon, especially after his performance at the 1974 World Cup with his native Holland.

Ten years on from a young Cruyff helping Ajax knock Liverpool out of the European Cup, the Dutchman was going to face them again. He wasn't a young talent now either. He was the finished article.

The first leg was held in Spain. John Toshack scored the only goal of the game to give them a precious lead to take back to Anfield. The home fans didn't take defeat well and started to throw cushions onto the pitch. They were disgusted and wanted to let their players know it. Some of the missiles landed a little bit too close to the Liverpool bench and one man in particular wasn't happy about it.

Joey Jones stood up and stared at the crowd as cushions continued to rain down all around the field. Joey was irate, he thought the home supporters were aiming for the Liverpool lads.

Joey started to pick up the cushions and began hurling them back at the Barcelona fans. He had to be pulled away and told to sit back down before something bad happened.

After the game, I queued to interview Johan Cruyff. He confidently told the listeners back home on Merseyside that things would be better in the second leg for Barcelona. After we finished the interview, I asked him if it was possible for me to come and talk to him on the day of the return match. He agreed.

I found out that the Barcelona squad would be based at the Holiday Inn in Liverpool, so on the morning of the second leg, I made my way there. Cruyff met me and we recorded a conversation between us both. He was absolutely brilliant and I was so happy.

It felt a bit of an empty gesture, but to say thanks I gave him a Radio City t-shirt for his two-year-old son. Little Jordi Cruyff later became a professional himself and played for Barcelona, Manchester United and Holland before taking on various roles in the game.

Johan Cruyff then explained that he had to pop somewhere but asked me if I could wait. Of course I could, but he was gone for a while, so I was thinking of packing up and leaving. It didn't look like he was coming back.

Just when I'd given up hope, he appeared. He presented me with a Barcelona tie and signed it for me. After my "gift" for him, he wanted to return the favour.

A Radio City t-shirt for a Barcelona tie signed by Johan Cruyff was a fair swap!

Johan Cruyff was an absolute gentleman but he couldn't influence the game enough to stop Liverpool progressing to the final. They'd now face Club Brugge of Belgium, who'd eliminated Hamburg in their semi-final.

For many years, the UEFA Cup Final was played over two legs, just like all the previous rounds. It was an interesting concept and meant that there was the jeopardy of away goals to contend with. Liverpool were to play at home first before going to Belgium three weeks later.

And the first leg was an absolute classic.

7

Bruges

People associate Anfield with big European nights. Flags, banners, scarves and a sea of noise. But in the first leg of the UEFA Cup Final against Club Brugge back in 1976, the place was in a state of shock. The Belgians raced into a two-nil lead after only fifteen minutes.

Anfield was stunned, but on the hour Ray Kennedy pulled one back. The noise level grew. Two minutes later, they were level through Jimmy Case. Anfield sensed victory. Then a penalty was given and Kevin Keegan scored.

So it was off to Bruges to commentate on the second leg with Liverpool holding a slender lead.

With the match being carried on various radio stations and of course TV, the Liverpool fans at home would soon have a reason to listen to us.

The reason was none other than Bill Shankly.

The appointment of Shanks proved to be a major coup. Terry Smith put full-page ads in the local papers on Merseyside. My name was in small letters, Bill's was highlighted in big bold text. It worked too.

The trip, however, was somewhat uncomfortable for him. He was kept well away from the players and staff. Bill had to stay in the same hotel as the wives. I was in the team hotel.

Arriving in Belgium in plenty of time for the game gave all the journalists the chance to let their hair down. The night before the match, a group of us decided to go out and explore. The game wasn't going to start until about 9pm the next day. We had plenty of time to recover. No sweat. So we went for it. We had a big night and nobody gave a shit about what time it was.

We had a few and I didn't get to bed until late. I wasn't worried, I could sleep in as long as I wanted. My work responsibilities wouldn't begin until late afternoon. I got to sleep but then I was woken by the phone in my room. I was knackered.

Who the hell was ringing me this early in the morning?

"Hello Elton son."

You guessed it.

"It's a b'aeutiful day. In Bruges. We shood see the sights."

"OK Bill, what time shall I pick you up?"

"In half an 'oor."

Oh shit!

I met up with Shanks and we explored Bruges. It was indeed a lovely day and we had a good walk around the place. Then Bill decided he wanted to go to the stadium. It was way too early and they were never going to let us in. They might not have opened up for me, but when Bill Shankly arrived, it was no issue at all. He was instantly recognised and welcomed into the ground.

We went through the gates and Shanks made a beeline for the pitch. It looked beautiful, especially as it was the end of the season. The turf was lush. The smell of the grass swept through the air. Bill looked down at it. He said nothing. He was surveying the field like an art expert would study a Van Gogh painting.

He turned to me and came out with one of the most blatantly obvious statements that I'd ever heard.

"Amazin' grass, son. It's green."

"What?"

Of course it was green. Bright green. If anyone else said it, you might laugh or scratch your head. But this was

Shanks. We stayed in the stadium and had a good look around. Slowly, fans started to appear for the match. We were hungry.

Thankfully the hot dog sellers in the ground were open for business. I went to buy one for me and Bill. These weren't just your standard hot dogs either. They were huge. I paid for them and made my way back around the pitch. At that moment, we heard a familiar accent.

"Alright Bill? How's it going?"

A few Liverpool fans had got into the stadium and were milling around. They couldn't believe their luck, bumping into Shanks. These lads were real Scousers too.

Being a man of the people, Bill was happy to chat with them about the match. This was long before mobile phones but one of the lads had a camera with him. Naturally they wanted their picture taken with the great man. They asked Bill to do his trademark clenched fist salute for them, which he'd done a thousand times before.

He'd never done it while holding a huge hot dog though. As Shanks squeezed his fist together, the sausage flew out of his hand and up into the air. It took off like a rocket. Ketchup and mustard dripped off it as it took flight.

Shanks didn't react. It was like it didn't even happen. I was pissing myself. Bill continued his conversation with the supporters instead. He paid no attention to what had just happened. The fans looked at me, before turning their attention back to Shanks.

"How did ye get 'ere, boys?"

They were nervous.

"Well Bill, errrr, first we got the train, errrr, hiding in the bogs. Then we hitchhiked a bit and, errrr, then bunked on another train."

Shanks couldn't believe it.

"Ye, ye've been, through a lot. I cannae have ye going back tae Liverpool like that."

Bill put his hand into his jacket pocket and pulled out a wad of notes. He handed them about eighty quid and told them to make sure that they got back safely. That was a lot of money in 1976.

It was a lovely gesture, especially as Bill was known for being frugal, shall we say. He'd made these lads so happy. They couldn't believe it. He wished them well for the game and their trip home and off they went.

As soon as they were out of earshot, Bill looked at me.

"Elton, son, the rest o' the day, is on ye. Ah dinae have a penny tae me name."

After what seemed like an eternity, the teams came out and the match started. Having Bill on co-commentary gave Radio City a massive share of the listeners. The volume was turned down on TV sets so people could listen to Shanks on Radio City.

The second leg finished 1-1, Liverpool had done it. Next up it was the big one; the European Cup.

It's during this run of matches that I'd draw more attention to my work and new opportunities would arise.

8

The road to Rome

Liverpool were back in the European Cup. Don't forget it was nothing like the Champions League is today. It was open to the league champions only, with one sole exception. The previous year's European Cup winners were also entered.

There was no seeding. It was a pure knock-out tournament, with each round played over two legs. It was wonderful and often so unpredictable. The big guns could meet at any moment. It also meant that champions from smaller countries could go further.

A straightforward victory over Crusaders from Northern Ireland in the first round got the ball rolling. Next up was Trabzonspor of Turkey, with the first leg over there. We had to go via Ankara, which in 1976 wasn't a pleasant place to be. Then it was off to Trabzon for the game. What happened during the match was not only ridiculous but unforgettable.

My commentary position was good. I was close to the pitch, with the connection going from Trabzon to Ankara before being sent to England. It'd been checked before the match and I was assured that everything was fine. The game was really tense and Liverpool weren't doing so well.

It wasn't live on TV, so the listeners were relying on me to paint a picture for them of what was happening. Things were reaching a crucial point when the phone rang in the home dugout. It was answered and there was a fair bit of noise, with some gesturing and waving going on. The ground was small, so I could see what was happening. It looked like they had a problem.

At that moment, Liverpool had a throw-in and Emlyn Hughes retrieved the ball from the sideline near the Turkish dugout. He could see me.

"Elt! Elt! There's a phone call for you!"

On the phone was my mate, Paul Davies. Paul went on to be a huge success in television and it was richly deserved. He was a great journalist and broadcaster. But before working for ITN, he was a colleague of mine at Radio City. And Paul was on the phone from the studio.

"Elton are you alright? We've not heard anything from you. There's no commentary!"

The feed from Turkey had stopped and the people back home had no idea what was going on. We were in deep shit. Or more like, I was. Paul had a solution though.

"Do it over the phone, and I'll put you on air."

Paul's quick-thinking meant that I could finish my commentary. But it was done from the Trabzonspor dugout. For the last twenty minutes, I commentated from an uncomfortable position down a phoneline on the home team's bench. It was amateur hour but at least I could relay the details back to Merseyside. Not that it was good news. Trabzonspor won 1-0.

I was furious and embarrassed by the whole situation. My boss Terry Smith was more livid than me. He had a right go. I don't know what else I could've done. The problem came somewhere between Turkey and England. Terry wanted someone to blame and I was made the scapegoat.

Liverpool won the return 3-0 at Anfield. They were through to the quarter-finals and would face St. Etienne. The French champions had narrowly lost to Bayern Munich in the 1976 final. Out in France for the first leg, the hosts were given a boost when their star player Dominique Rocheteau was declared fit.

Rocheteau was being compared to George Best, but he wasn't a patch on George. Rocheteau played with a swagger, with his long hair and pin-up image. It was more because of his image than his talent that people used the Bestie comparison.

For Liverpool, the team news was the total opposite. Kevin Keegan, who was a household name by now, missed out. One player who caught my eye though was Dominique Bathenay. It was his goal that separated the two sides when the whistle went for the end of the first leg.

Liverpool just had to do the business at Anfield. What happened next? It remains one of the most incredible European nights at Anfield. And for me personally, it became a springboard for the next step in my career. Ironically, I didn't want to do the game. I wanted to be in Sheffield.

On the very same night was the League Cup final replay between Everton and Aston Villa at Hillsborough. Despite it being a final, Liverpool in the European Cup took priority for Terry and Radio City. I had no choice. I was off to Anfield.

Kevin Keegan was back from injury and his presence in the team gave those around the club a lift. It didn't take him long to make his mark either. Picking up the ball from a corner on the left, he floated the ball into the net. Was it a cross? The home fans didn't care.

It was still 1-0 at half-time and the tension was growing in the stands. Then early into the second half, Bathenay shrugged off Jimmy Case and sent a swerving shot from about thirty yards past Ray Clemence and into the net. It had to be something special to beat Ray from there. Bathenay had scored again and now Liverpool needed two goals, because of the away goal rule.

Within eight minutes, Ray Kennedy put the hosts 2-1 up. One goal needed and around half an hour to get it. The Kop was swaying back and forth, urging their heroes forward. The volume had risen even more.

The clock was ticking and it looked like Liverpool might just fall short. Replacing John Toshack in attack, David Fairclough had been introduced with about fifteen minutes to go. He had already been dubbed "Supersub" because of his ability to come off of the bench and score.

Had he got another one in him?

There were six minutes to go when Fairclough raised the roof off of Anfield. He controlled a long ball and raced clear, shooting into the net at the Kop end. The scenes were hard to put in words. I described the goal, and without realising, my words would be remembered for years to come. It has always been a huge compliment for me when people recall what I said.

The commentary went something like this:

"Liverpool playing too many long balls, too many hopeful balls. And there's another, which has broken for...FAIRCLOUGH...!!!"

I'm very proud of my career, and what happened at Anfield that night is part of it. Phil Thompson was missing from the first XI that night. Out through injury, his only way to follow the game from hospital was through Radio City. He fell out of bed celebrating Fairclough's winner! He can still recite what I said for that crucial goal. A goal which almost defined my career on Radio City.

Liverpool were never in any danger in the semi-final against FC Zurich. The Swiss side struggled badly and the Reds won both legs. Bob Paisley had done what Shanks couldn't. He'd got Liverpool to a European Cup final. I had to pinch myself. I was almost twenty-six and I'd be commentating on the European Cup final. I couldn't believe how far I'd come in such a short time.

I've been asked many times by other Everton supporters what it was like to be there for this era of Liverpool's domination. I saw it as business. I wanted to further my career.

Working for Radio City and being the voice of Liverpool's games was the perfect platform for me to get noticed. I could've been the best commentator in the world working for Radio Cumbria covering Carlisle United, but nobody would have ever heard of me.

Without these Liverpool games, I might not have worked in television. I have to be honest, I wanted Liverpool to win the European Cup. That's because I wanted to be the commentator synonymous with that success. Not only that, the youngest.

Liverpool had been chasing the treble but their dreams ended in the FA Cup final at the hands of Manchester United, just four days before the European Cup final. Liverpool had been strong favourites but after wrapping up the title, they'd been accused of taking the foot off the gas. They didn't win any of their last four league games.

Before one of those fixtures, away to Coventry, I was sat in the reception of the hotel where the team had checked in. The plan was for the players to have an afternoon nap. Kevin Keegan and David Johnson walked by and invited me to their room to watch horse racing, which I did.

Their main topic of conversation was the Coventry game. They were motivated to put on a show for their fans. They didn't strike me as complacent at all. The criticism of Liverpool was unjustified.

After Manchester United's 2-1 win at Wembley, I was happy for my good friend Steve Coppell, who later became the godfather to my son Chris. I was also concerned about the impact on the Liverpool lads. You could imagine the psychological damage of losing the FA Cup final.

I went to the dressing room for an interview. Bob appeared and invited me in. Understandably, there was a real sombre atmosphere. The younger players like Casey and Joey Jones looked devastated. Bob told me to interview Ray Clemence and insisted that everyone heard Ray's words.

Clem answered my questions loudly. He spoke about this being a minor setback and how it would inspire the team to go to Rome and win the European Cup. The rest of the lads sat there open-mouthed. Clem's rallying call had the right effect. When the team left the changing room, the mood had swung. It was extraordinary.

As I left the room, Bob Paisley looked at me and gave me a wink.

"Do you want me next son?"

Liverpool were ready for Rome.

And so was I.

9

From Rome to Manchester

I headed over to Italy and was in the same hotel as the players and staff again. After doing a piece for the station, I was now free until the next day, when the final would take place. I wandered downstairs and in the bar were Sir John Smith and Peter Robinson.

Sir John ran the club's off-field activities alongside Peter. We made some small talk about the game before I asked where Bob Paisley was. I hadn't seen him for a while. Apparently, he'd gone to his room but had been down earlier that evening.

The two club officials had asked Bob what his plans were and he told them that he was off to have a look at Rome. He wanted to retrace his steps from the Second World War! The last time he'd been to Rome, he arrived on a tank in 1945. Peter and Sir John explained that it wasn't a good idea; the city was full of Liverpool fans.

The next day, Liverpool lifted their first European Cup, winning 3-1 against Borussia Mönchengladbach. At 2-1 up and with only seven minutes to go, Liverpool were awarded a penalty. Phil Neal took it and scored. As the ball nestled into the net, I made a statement that thankfully I got away with.

"And Liverpool have won the European Cup!"

I was being presumptuous, but's that how it felt. So after a slight pause, there was only one word that I could think of.

"Surely."

When everyone returned to the hotel, there was a party atmosphere. Bob was in great form. Someone said to him "Paisley conquers Europe".

Quick as a flash, Bob responded:

"You know what happened to the last fella who tried to do that!"

Then in front of us all, he swept his hair to one side and took a comb out of his pocket. He stuck it under his nose and impersonated Hitler. Everyone was in stitches. It became his party piece.

The pressure of a long season was off and Bob was able to relax, safe in the knowledge that he'd made history. Despite normally enjoying a whisky, Bob didn't touch a drop of alcohol after the game. I offered to get him one, but he politely refused. He explained that he wanted to savour every moment.

It's a good job Bob did like whisky, he won that many Bell's Manager of the Month Awards, he had an endless supply of huge bottles of the stuff. He even gave one to me once. I was delighted for Bob personally that Liverpool won that night.

There weren't many people during the different moments of my career that I considered as mentors. Bob Paisley was one.

After the huge success of 1976/77, the big story coming out of the club was the departure of Kevin Keegan. He was off to West Germany to play for Hamburger SV. Kevin was promised a huge increase in salary. He was seen as being the type of player that could put the club at the top of the tree in the Bundesliga and ultimately Europe. His transfer fee was a British record.

It just underlined even further how much of a star Kevin was. I was sad to see him go.

I spent a lot of time with him during my Radio City days. Kevin was such a good man. He had a lot of charisma and a great sense of humour. We did an event at Russell's Club in the city and the crowd loved him. It was Parkinson style.

One on one with a microphone each. We had Gerry Marsden as the first guest to warm up the audience.

The event went longer than planned. We finished about midnight but that wasn't the end. Kevin stayed until around 1.30am, signing autographs, having his photo taken with the fans and chatting to them all.

Although he was a superstar, Kevin had never forgotten his roots. His wife Jean was with him, watching her husband with HIS people. Kevin, like Johan Cruyff, proved to me that often the bigger they are, the nicer they are. But going to Hamburg was, in his words, a massive challenge.

And by the end of that year, I'd be in a similar position.

Being at Radio City, people were hearing my work and my reputation was growing. The St. Etienne match was cited as the one that made people sit up and take notice.

You never know who's aware of you or what you do. And that proved to be the case.

Before that, the new season arrived and I was back on commentary duty covering Liverpool. On the first day of the campaign in August, I was off to Middlesbrough aboard the team bus. The man signed to replace Kevin Keegan was about to make his debut.

Arriving from Celtic, Kenny Dalglish took Keegan's number seven shirt and never looked back. Liverpool weren't going to rest on their laurels. I'd continue covering their league games too. This was when I first met someone who'd later become one of my closest friends in football. It was all thanks to Joe Fagan.

Middlesbrough's former boss was at Ayresome Park to watch the side he walked away from earlier that year. He was a World Cup winner and from one of football's most famous families. I'm sure he didn't remember our first encounter but I certainly did.

Joe introduced me to Jack Charlton.

After the final whistle, I had to finish my report on the Middlesbrough game. It ended 1-1 with Kenny scoring. He'd instantly adapted to life as a Liverpool player.

I mentioned before the respect that Liverpool's players and staff showed me. This was never more apparent when I was late for the team bus back to Anfield. Due to my media commitments, everyone was sat on the coach except one person; me.

Bob Paisley insisted that they wait.

I arrived and apologised sheepishly, as the players greeted me with ironic cheers. Bob eventually joined me. He asked me for my thoughts on the game. I told him that I was impressed with a particular player for Middlesbrough; Graeme Souness. Bob then explained that he rated Souness very highly and that Liverpool would be signing him in the near future.

My eyes lit up. What an exclusive!

I couldn't use it.

Bob explained that he was telling me in total confidence. The journalist side of me was disappointed that I couldn't use the scoop. On a personal level, I was flattered that Bob saw me as someone he could trust with confidential information such as that.

In January 1978, Graeme Souness was officially unveiled as a Liverpool player.

Bob Paisley then gave me something else and he was sure I could use it.

Don Revie had quit as England boss and Ron Greenwood had taken over as caretaker manager. The former West Ham boss got the gig full time later that year.

Greenwood had told Bob that he intended calling up all of Liverpool's English players and starting them for the game against Switzerland. This included veteran Ian Callaghan. Cally hadn't played for his country since the 1966 World Cup!

Oddly though, there was one exception. Jimmy Case wasn't going to get a call up, despite being in great form.

Bob had no problem with his players being chosen. He also had no issue telling me about his discussion with Greenwood either. I was itching to break the story before Greenwood spilled it to the London media.

Then Bob had a doubt. He asked for some time to speak with Ron Greenwood, to make certain that it was fine for me to report it. I was ready to use the story. I knew it would be huge. Bob assured me that he'd have an answer by Monday. When the Sunday papers came out, there was no sign of the story. It appeared that I was the only one who had this exclusive.

I went to see Bob on the Monday, as I'd planned. When I got to his office, he asked me why I was there. I told him it was about the Greenwood story and he apologised. He'd forgotten to ask Ron Greenwood. Bob told me not to worry and said it would be alright to break the news.

So I did.

This revelation was the main news story all day. It didn't matter what else was happening in the area, the Ron Greenwood story was the first thing that each bulletin began with on Radio City.

Word travelled fast.

The next morning, it was the back page headline in all the national papers. I think it was the Daily Express who had the best one:

"Ron Kops the lot"

As the year headed towards its close, my time at Radio City was also coming to an end. No more cigars with Bob Paisley. No more team bus scoops. My dream of working on television was about to become a reality, as the result of another surprise phone call. This time an exciting opportunity came to me. I didn't have to go looking for it or seize the moment. No running to a phone box this time.

My future lay at Granada Television. Granada was and still is the TV franchise covering the North West of England. Incorporating both Liverpool and the company's home city of Manchester for ITV, it has produced some of the best television over the years. Its biggest success? Coronation Street. It might not be everyone's cup of tea but it's been on the air since 1960.

Moving jobs meant that I met a man who became an ally, a mentor and most of all a good friend. Paul "The Doc" Doherty was THE man at Granada Television and he wanted me to join the team. Paul had begun as a freelance reporter and worked himself up. From being a producer, he became the head of sport at Granada and was highly regarded within the company.

Paul was an innovator and extremely protective of his employees. If you were loyal to him and did a good job, Paul made sure that everything went smoothly for you. I'll talk about The Doc a lot more. From now on, I'll mainly call him The Doc or The Chief.

Without Paul Doherty, I'd never have had the career in television that I had.

Paul had heard enough of my work to be convinced that I was the right man to employ. He then did his due diligence before offering me a job. Paul was thorough. He wanted to be sure that he wasn't hiring someone with dark secrets, a shady past or extra-curricular activities that might have spelled trouble.

Before that though, I had to tie up my loose ends at Radio City. I went to David Maker, the man who hired me in the first place and explained that I couldn't refuse the offer. He understood and was brilliant about everything. He had a ready-made replacement for me; Clive Tyldesley.

I hired Clive not long before leaving for Granada. Richard Keys joined Radio City to work with Clive. It wouldn't be too long before Keysie and I were collaborating together either. When Richard was commentating on games for Radio City, he'd ask me to join him as a co-commentator. We became pals.

It was a wrench to leave Radio City. The station and its people had done so much for me.

Leaving Radio City also coincided with the birth of my first child. Joyce gave birth to Christopher in January 1978 and in the bed next to her was Mick Lyons' wife. Despite the arrival of our babies, Mick still came to my leaving party at the Holiday Inn.

Clive organised it all and did it "This Is Your Life" style. Wally smuggled Joyce out of the hospital. What a surprise!

Clive also presented an audio clip for me.

"Elton, there's someone who can't be with us tonight. But he's sent a message for you. Do you recognise this voice?"

Clive started the tape. It was someone very familiar to me.

"Hullo son."

It was Bill Shankly.

"Ah like what ye've done for Radio City. That's why they've chosen ye. Ye have the voice for radio. An' the face for TV."

That meant a lot to me. The leaving party was never going to be his scene. Too much booze, not enough tea!

So much was happening in my life. I'd worked at the newspaper and gained brilliant experience. Afterwards, I'd spent over three years at Radio City.

It was time to be on the telly.

10

A face for TV

My first day at Granada arrived and I got down to business. And it was hard. I had to do a lot behind the scenes. There was not one single microphone in my hand. No cameras were pointed at me either. I didn't expect my new job to be like this. I had visions of being on TV instantly. It wasn't panning out that way. I was being groomed for better things, I just didn't realise it at the time.

To be honest, it got me down. After about six months working there, if I'd been offered the chance to go back to Radio City, I'd have taken it. Finally, my efforts and a lot of patience paid off. I got my chance. I'd be doing the sports report from the studio as part of Granada Reports. It would go out live too.

This was shortly after the 1978 World Cup in Argentina, won by the hosts under the management of the charismatic, chain-smoking César Luis Menotti.

One of the main presenters for the programme that day was the one and only Tony Wilson. Not only was he a brilliant journalist, but he became even more famous for his work in the music industry and the Hacienda nightclub in Manchester.

And Tony decided to introduce me in style.

"Today, we have a new sports reporter."

He paused.

"We tried to get César Luis Menotti."

He was grinning.

"He couldn't do it."

He began reeling off a list of unattainable names, from the sublime to the ridiculous.

Time for the punchline.

"Instead, we've ended up with Elton John. Sorry Welsby!"

"Over to you Elton."

Welcome to live TV!

Now throughout my time on radio and TV, I was always good at improvising. It came naturally. I looked straight at the camera. This was my first time on air. And it was live across the North West. I just had to try and equal Tony's witty intro.

"I'd just like to say that Tony Wilson prepared that gag, at my expense, during the two and a half hours he spent in makeup before the show."

How was he going to take it?

Tony howled laughing. He had no problem with me giving him some back. Tony's other presenter, Granada icon and stalwart Bob Greaves was also pissing himself. I think both of them could be heard at home.

Tony and I became a double act. If there was something to cover with a sporting interest, we'd do it together. These stories often took us out of the office and would be a lot of fun.

Despite being a proud Mancunian, the man later labelled as "Mr Manchester" would have to travel to Merseyside too. We'd rib each other about that. And it's there that the man I called "Willo" got a painful surprise.

We were in Kirkby to interview an attractive young lady, who also happened to be a martial arts champion. Of course, there was some laughing and joking between the three of us. Until I whispered to "Bruce Lee":

"Don't hold back".

She took him out with a kick to his midriff. He hit the deck in agony. That clip still gets played today when Granada remembers Tony.

I was the lucky one there and the same happened when the two of us visited Lancashire Country Cricket Club. They'd just bought a new bowling machine and I was interviewing David "Bumble" Lloyd about it. I asked "Bumble" if my mate could have a go with the machine.

Cue Tony.

Willo came out in full cricket whites, ready for action. Now we could have some fun.

"Does this go up to 100 mph?" I asked Bumble.

"Sure, no problem."

So he set the machine to that speed. Tony had no idea. He was waiting, bat in hand, to face a delivery. The machine launched the ball, as fast as lightning. I'd never seen anything like it.

The ball flew between the bat and his hip. Tony didn't even see it. I was so relieved it didn't hit him. But it was a close one. David Lloyd still remembers the story to this day.

Tony Wilson was excellent at his job and is sorely missed. He died of cancer in 2007. He was only 57. He left a massive legacy and influenced many. His fingerprints are all over Manchester, the North West and especially Granada.

At the time, we had the Friday night football show "Kick Off". It's fondly remembered in the region. The channel's main football man was Gerald Sinstadt. I joined the show and my role at first was to work as a reporter and do voiceovers.

My first assignment was at Preston North End. I had to go in goal and face penalties from Alex Bruce (not Steve's son). A man of my height isn't cut out to be a keeper. But I put on all the kit and faced up to Alex, who had a phenomenal record from the spot.

He scored five out five.

So he took a sixth.

Saved!

I think Alex took pity on me with that effort.

When the footage was shown, Gerald Sinstadt said about me: "If anyone wants him, we're open to offers". The Doc thought it was a snide dig. He made it clear to Gerry that you never undermine a colleague. Gerry saw me as a threat. Pure and simple. I suppose he was right.

We also had "Kick Off Match", where we covered the highlights of the local North West clubs. Other ITV regions did the same.

Gerry had been established with Granada for a long time and he commentated on these matches as well. His voice was unmistakeable. Co-presenting with Gerry prepared me for the future, when it would be my time to fly solo.

Before becoming the main host, I'd also do voiceovers for the short clips, rounding up the action. At the very beginning, there were two of us doing it. The other was Ian St. John. The both us would sit in front of a monitor and narrate the goals from the midweek games. We covered teams from the old Second, Third and Fourth Divisions.

I also managed to commentate on a couple of matches myself, but through unfortunate circumstances. Gerry went down with a bout of Bell's Palsy. If you're not familiar with the condition, it's facial paralysis. It's like you've had a stroke. You can't control part of your face and often your mouth. There was no way he could be on camera. His voice was affected too.

I took over as main presenter and also commentator for two games. The first was Everton versus Bristol City. You couldn't write the script. My first TV commentary and at my spiritual home, Goodison Park. The late Andy King scored a hat trick.

Andy was a cracking lad, albeit a bit scatterbrained. There was a summer fete at my son Chris's school and I was asked if I could get someone to open it. I asked Andy. No problem. He had no idea where to go and there was no sat nav at the time. I arranged to meet him at Arrowe Park Hospital. Then I got in his car and navigated from there.

It was a beautiful, red hot day for the summer fete. I got into the passenger seat next to Andy and we set off. Within a moment or two, I started to sweat. The temperature in the car was really high. It was becoming unbearable.

"Can you put some cool air on please Andy?"

"It's already on."

"Are you sure? It's boiling in here."

"That'll be me heated seats. Don't know how to turn 'em off."

Now back to business.

The second match I did was Manchester United against Arsenal. Alan Sunderland scored two goals in an away win. The Doc complimented me on adjusting to television commentary. He never asked me again.

Gerry only missed those two commentaries but it was a good few weeks before he returned to present Kick Off. When he did, a significant change was made. As I didn't use it, The Doc told Gerry that he'd no longer be working with autocue. Gerry wasn't happy about it but The Doc was adamant. Plus, it saved the sports department money.

The Doc thought Gerry's time was up, both as a presenter and a commentator.

Gerald Sinstadt left Granada in 1981. Martin Tyler came from Yorkshire TV and stepped in to take over the commentary duties. Gerry's career continued elsewhere. First, he went to Southern Television, covering teams like Southampton and Brighton. Later, he went to the BBC.

We lost Gerry in 2021. He was 91.

Kick Off had access to all the local clubs in the Granada region. The Doc had so many ideas how we could be different. He was so highly respected in football. The Doc's dad Peter Doherty played for Blackpool, Manchester City and Doncaster Rovers. He was also Northern Ireland manager for eleven years.

The Chief was great friends with Malcolm Allison, who was managing Manchester City around this time. "Big Mal" was a larger-than-life character and had been assistant manager at Manchester City during their success at the end of the 1960s. Now he was THE boss at Maine Road.

He was flamboyant and loved the good life. He wore big coats, large hats, smoked cigars and loved a drink.

Allison also loved the ladies. But he didn't love me. From the first moment I met him, we didn't hit it off. I have no idea why.

One of the players coached by Allison at Manchester City when they won the title in 1968 was Alan Oakes. He was now player/manager of Chester City. Oakes tipped off Allison about Ian Rush, who he thought was going to be a star and would score goals at the highest level. Oakes told Big Mal to move quickly because of interest from elsewhere.

Allison said he'd pop down and take a look at Rush if he had time.

If he had time!!!

Allison never went to see Rush play. He never followed up on the advice that Alan Oakes gave him. Sorry, City fans.

You know what happened next. Liverpool scouted Rush and signed him.

The rest is history.

The Chief didn't just have his friendship with Allison. He had brilliant relationships with lots of managers, players and directors. So much so that he was able to convince them to do anything.

And I'm not exaggerating either.

One year, we had a Christmas choir singing carols. Nothing out of the ordinary there. Except the singers were all players from the area. Just imagine it? One current player from each of the seventeen clubs in the Granada region including Lou Macari, Mick Channon and eventual two-time European Cup winner Alan Kennedy. It was thought to be an impossible task to get all of them, but we managed it.

The choir closed the show with a well-known Christmas carol, conducted by Jimmy Armfield.

We went even further when we did the Kick Off Pantomime, introduced by none other than Denis Law. "The King" was loved in Manchester, having played for both City and United. He also worked alongside me on Kick Off and MatchTime. Denis was great to work with.

Of course, we followed the traditional panto rules, which meant men dressed up as women. Starting with the Ugly Sisters. Except these were played by two goalkeepers!

Joe Corrigan and Jim "Seamus" McDonagh left their day jobs behind and put on dresses – and an enormous amount of makeup so they could do their roles justice.

If you think that was something else, imagine Widow Twanky played by none other than Bryan Robson. The man who had commanded the biggest transfer fee at the time.

Dressed as a pantomime dame! The three of them were unrecognisable. They looked so authentic.

We also had Ian Rush as Dick Whittington. Malcolm Allison knew who he was by then!

The Doc was behind it all. He was close to so many people. They didn't hesitate to say yes, despite it being outlandish. I mean this in a positive way; he was a hard man to say no to.

The programme was renowned throughout football, so even those from outside the Granada region were happy to appear. Managers or coaches who were playing in the North West on the Saturday would come to the studios on Friday evening to be interviewed.

One stands out in particular. Sir Alf Ramsey, the mastermind behind England's World Cup win in 1966.

Sir Alf had recently left his job as manager of Birmingham City. The interview was exactly as you'd expect. We talked about English football's finest hour and how he found life at Birmingham. He spoke well but there were no exclusives or headlines for the following day's papers.

Sir Alf was hardly a sensationalist like Clough or Allison. After the show, we adjourned to the green room for drinks and everyone's opinion of the show plus how we should follow it up the next week.

Sir Alf just listened, intently, sipping a small glass of sherry. After about an hour, he still hadn't left. The Doc and I both enquired if he was okay and he just held his hand up and said "Fine, thank you for asking".

Then all of a sudden, he stood up, coughed to get our attention, cleared his throat and made a speech. He basically said how much he appreciated being invited to appear on the show he'd heard so much about. He praised our professionalism and obvious love for football and thanked us again for our generous hospitality.

You could've heard a pin drop.

In fact, some of the production team just stood there with their mouths wide open when he was speaking. It only lasted a couple of minutes before he wished us all goodnight and left. Doc shot after him and guided him to the car park while we all just looked at each other in amazement.

We felt privileged that England's legendary World Cup manager had paid us a visit; he felt privileged to have been invited.

Another visitor to the Kick Off studio was the highly controversial Burnley chairman, Bob Lord. He'd become acting president of the Football League in 1981 and among his targets were the press and television. He didn't seem to care what he said or who offended.

With all this in mind, it should've been a lively interview. But Mr Lord had one condition before accepting our invitation.

"I want to meet that Ena Sharples."

Doc said he'd see what he could do. The next step was to contact the executive producer of Coronation Street, Bill Podmore. In those days, the cast of "The Street" weren't allowed to do any outside work, so we couldn't go directly to Violet Carson who played Ena. Podmore agreed as long as it was okay with Miss Carson.

It was, so the Friday night in question, Lord arrived at about 6pm. Violet Carson was being looked after by Ursula Cockburn, the show's production assistant. In his blunt Lancashire manner, Lord insisted that he wanted to meet Ena Sharples.

Ursula said that Miss Carson would be with him in a minute.

"I don't wanna meet no Miss Carson, I'm 'ere to meet Ena Sharples!"

People seemed to believe in "The Street". When the character Minnie Caldwell "died" in the show, wreathes were laid outside the Granada building in Quay Street.

It beggars belief. It's a soap opera!

11

Goodbye Bill

Tuesday 29th September 1981 should've been like any other day. But, on this day, British football was rocked with devastating news.

You've already gathered how I feel about Bill Shankly. I probably could've just written a book about him alone. What is difficult to put into words though is how I reacted to the news, that in the early hours of the morning of Tuesday 29th September 1981, Mr William Shankly OBE died. It hit me hard. He was 68.

I wasn't the only one to have difficulty processing the information.

Shanks didn't touch alcohol. Offer Bill a cup of tea and he was happy. Give him a second one, and he was even happier. He wouldn't say no to a third or fourth either. Bill kept himself fit. He regularly played five-a-side football in a sports hall near his home.

Yet three days before, he'd been admitted to Broadgreen Hospital in Liverpool after a heart attack. As soon as people knew he was there, they came in numbers and waited outside for information. On the Monday, his condition worsened. For once, the man with a winning mentality, who never knew when he was beaten, couldn't fight any longer.

It didn't feel real.

The Doc made the decision immediately. He wanted us to get a tribute show out that day. Paul was brilliant like that. He also had the influence and network to make sure that it would be the best one possible. Not that anyone would need much convincing to be part of it. Bill Shankly's fingerprints were all over football. He was adored by

Liverpool fans and highly respected elsewhere too. Inside the game, he'd influenced so many people.

Calls were made and the invited accepted without hesitation. Everyone was able to make it. Not one person was unavailable. A green room was quickly prepared for when the guests arrived, with unlimited sandwiches and drinks. By the time everyone came, the room was full of some of the biggest names in football.

I conducted interviews with everyone throughout the day. They were recorded to be part of the programme, to be aired later. There would be no match action, just tributes. The understated opening titles were intentional.

Beginning a TV special about the death of someone that I knew so well wasn't a pleasant experience. I was also using autocue. It was my first time doing so. With such an emotional occasion, I was glad of it. I didn't write the script, that task was assigned to John Roberts of The Daily Mail. I didn't speak for too long before I passed over to Denis Law.

When "The Lawman" played for Huddersfield Town in the 1950s, Bill Shankly was his boss. Denis explained how Bill turned average players into good ones and good ones into world beaters. He then told a story about a conversation he had with Shanks about coaching.

This was Bill's advice to Denis:

"Coaching? I'll tell you about coaching. You go to the FA Coaching Course at Lilleshall for two weeks. Come back and do the exact opposite of what they told you to do and you'll be successful. That's coaching."

Bill Shankly had the wisdom to appreciate the value of an individualist and the wit to get the best out of him. Denis Law had a wonderful career and there's no doubt that his early dealings with Bill Shankly helped him.

Ian St. John was next. "The Saint" had been there for the transformation of Liverpool under Bill and he was proud to be part of it. When we spoke, he seemed in shock. Ian wasn't taking it all in. He lifted the lid on some of Bill's man management style.

"When teams from London came to Anfield, he'd stand outside their dressing room and then told us they looked pale and tired, probably after a night on the town.

He tried to psyche out the opposition and on many occasions he succeeded. He used those tactics in Europe too. Before we played Anderlecht once, he decided we'd play in all red. Shirts, shorts and socks. So intimidating.

He didn't just want us to be fit, he wanted us to be super fit. When the press used to ask what the team was the following day he'd say 'the same as last season'."

Speaking to people like Denis and Ian made reality bite. None of us ever expected Shanks to die. He felt immortal. Another example of Bill's psychological edge was the famous "This is Anfield" sign, which he was responsible for. He was ahead of his time. With so many people at Granada paying homage to him, the spirit of Shankly felt as present as ever.

By now, Kevin Keegan had returned to England and was playing for Southampton. As he had a match that night, Kevin couldn't be with us in Manchester. He was able to join us from a studio on the South Coast though. Kevin has always been an emotional person and it must've been very difficult for him to appear on camera. Shanks took him from the Fourth Division and helped him become a superstar.

With tears in his eyes, Kevin opened up about his old boss.

"He never lost his verve for the game. I consider myself fortunate to have seen him two weeks ago at Manchester City and we had a good chat. I never thought it would be the last time. I think I got as close to him as any footballer. I would just hope and pray that Liverpool Football Club will do something to honour his memory. There should have been a throne in the directors' box for him. I'm sure they must be thinking about something because he built that club."

Eleven months later, Bill's widow Ness unlocked the Shankly Gates at Anfield. The tribute that Kevin asked for was official.

A lot of people, understandably because of their age, probably don't realise what Bill inherited when he first came to Merseyside in 1959. This was not the Liverpool Football Club that people know today. Shanks described Anfield as an eyesore. The club was in the Second Division. Despite the challenge in front of him, Bill saw potential. That gave him a foundation to build on.

His great rival during the 1960s and very early 1970s was Harry Catterick. Whereas Shanks was an extrovert, Harry was the opposite. Despite their rivalry, Harry came to Manchester to do the show.

Here's what Harry had to say:

"I bumped into him one day outside Bellefield, our training ground. Bill's house overlooked where we trained every day.

'Have ye seen the centre half A've just signed?'

'No I haven't Bill. He's a Dundee lad isn't he?'

'Aye. Ah could play Arthur Askey in goal wi' him there!'

I shall miss him. Miss the many chats we had at various grounds when we met up going to watch the same match. He was very dear to everyone on Merseyside. In all my time there as a player and manager I've never known anyone so loved."

That centre half Bill told Harry about was Ron Yeats, signed in 1961 from Dundee United. Yeats was quickly appointed captain. He had the perfect attitude for a Bill Shankly team and Yeats appreciated his boss for his man-management skills.

The interview with Yeats was up next.

"He was the best motivator I ever knew. Ian Callagan was 5'6" and the doorway to Shanks' office was 6'6". Cally could hardly fit through it after a pep talk from the boss.

On one occasion, one of the lads was injured and saw a specialist. He told Bill he'd be out for a month.

'A month?!!' he exclaimed.

Shanks immediately rang the specialist and said 'we're not dealin' wi' human beings here, son'."

One man who Shanks looked up to was Tom Finney. They played together at Preston, and Finney had no problem coming to do the tribute show for his old mate. Finney was Bill's hero, no two ways about it. Shanks would have loved what Tom Finney said about him.

"I came into the Preston team during the war and we won the wartime Cup and League. Bill played behind me at right half. And let me say he played as he managed, full of energy and enthusiasm. He was a great inspiration to me."

I mentioned before that if Bill wasn't in the best of moods when we picked him up to do some work at Radio City, then we'd have to find a subject that would ease the tension. One day I found that Tom Finney was the sweet spot. Bill went sort of misty eyed as he started to talk about his hero.

"He was like Best an Cruyff rolled intae one. He had pace an' incredible control of the ball. Defenders couldnae nick the ball off him 'cause it wis inches frae his feet."

I asked him how Finney compared to Sir Stanley Matthews, football's first Knight, and widely regarded as the greatest player of his generation. Sir Stanley played until he was 50.

"Nae comparison, son. Stan wis a good player. He'd beat the left half, run oan an' beat a coverin' player, then beat the left back an' cross the ball. He very rarely scored. Tom wid beat a player, maybe two, then cut inside an' go at the heart o' the defence an' most likely score wi' either foot. He wis fuckin' fantastic, son."

On one famous occasion when Shanks visited Deepdale for a game against Sheffield United, Tony Currie had a great game for the visitors. Afterwards, with the press swarming round Bill, a local journalist asked Bill how Currie compared to Finney.

Shanks replied in typical fashion.

"He played weel. As good as Finney? Maybe so. But ye've got tae bear in mind Tom's 60."

His razor like wit was there after he retired and up until the day he died. He always had a one liner. Not nasty, just funny. Wherever he went on his footballing travels from 1974 onwards, all the press wanted to know what he thought about the game. The respect for him was off the charts. I saw that most notably at Tranmere.

He was a consultant there for a brief spell just advising Johnny King whenever Kingy asked for it. Bill had been observing for a while as Tranmere were going through a mediocre spell. Kingy asked him whether to switch to a 4-4-2 or a 4-3-3 and Shanks gave Kingy his honest opinion.

"Naw. Where ye're goin' wrong is in trainin'. Ye go tae the Bebington Oval. Change. Train. Shower. Change. An' then ye go home. Naw, son. Ye should be goin' tae Prenton Park. Change. Get a coach tae trainin' an' then come back tae the ground afore goin' home."

So they followed Bill's advice. And went on a winning streak. They went through the exact same routine at Anfield. They changed at the ground then went to Melwood and trained. Afterwards they'd have a cup of tea then get the coach back to Anfield. They'd have a bath or shower then get dressed and go home.

One day, Brian Hall told me that they went through the first part of that routine, but when they got to Melwood, Shanks just told them all to soak in the bath and then get back on the coach. No explanation. To Shanks it just seemed like the right thing to do at the time. He was so idiosyncratic. He did everything his way. And he was never questioned. He had the success to back it up.

One man who really struggled with the sad news was Sir Matt Busby. As soon as Bill's death was confirmed, the Old Trafford switchboard received call after call, wanting his thoughts. Sir Matt would not take one of them.

Except from Paul Doherty.

Once Busby knew about the tribute, he wanted to be part of it. Not only were Sir Matt and Bill great friends, but Busby recommended Shanks to Liverpool. When he spoke that day about his old friend, he was visibly shaken. Yes, Sir Matt raised a glass of whisky or two to Bill but it was his emotions that got the better of him that day, not the Scotch.

As I listened to all these people recall their wonderful memories, I thought back myself. I spent so much time with Bill, often just the two of us. I still think of him today, and many a time I laugh to myself as a random memory comes back to me. I'm often asked about Shanks. He was a fascinating figure.

It really annoys me when modern day journalists and pundits toast Klopp as the best Liverpool manager ever. Without Bill, there wouldn't have been Klopp. Liverpool might have stayed as a club outside of the top-flight. We'll never know.

Regarding Bill Shankly, I have my own regrets though.

If I was working at a game, my time was always precious because I had a strict timetable to follow. Every second counted. After Bill retired, I'd often see him at different matches.

It breaks my heart to say this. I'd avoid him. Before you judge me, please let me explain why.

It wasn't because I didn't want to see him. I thought the world of him. It was because if he saw me, he'd stop me and talk for ages. It'd be almost impossible to get my work done. I'd go another way.

On the odd occasion that he spotted me, he'd smile, wave and beckon me over. With a friendly "Elton son!" he'd then start talking about the match. I'd always find it difficult to make my excuses and leave. I didn't want to disrespect him. I just had a job to do. I still feel terrible about it.

Bill helped me personally and professionally. He invited me into his home and treated me really well.

I'll never forget him.

12

Espana 82

When I watched England leave the field at the World Cup in 1970, heads bowed down following an extra-time elimination to West Germany, I couldn't have imagined that the country wouldn't play in the competition again until 1982. I also could never have envisaged that I'd be at the tournament in a working capacity either.

Thanks to The Doc, I was able to get better and better on Granada. Of course, I was still young and a little naïve. If I rewatch the shows from back then, I can't believe how young I look. I had a twinkle in my eye though! After Gerald Sinstadt left, I became the main man on Kick Off. And because The Chief had a lot of influence outside of our region, I was able to get other opportunities too.

The Doc was respected by most and feared by some. The ones that didn't like him were just jealous. He was so good. They wanted to keep The Doc at arm's length because they knew given the chance, he'd take over.

Doc'd make everything better, which would make them look bad. And I was his protégé. He went into bat for me so many times and he helped me to get on network TV. I believed that I was good enough, I just needed some assistance managing the politics.

And that was a minefield.

Having already done match reports for World of Sport when at Radio City, I wasn't totally unknown. But when the chance came up to be part of the ITV team for the World Cup in Spain, I knew that the door was open to bigger things. The Doc had my back as always but his adversaries saw me as part of HIS team. That didn't always work in my favour. I was Doc's "boy". There were certain people who would've taken great pleasure in me falling flat on my backside.

The "London Mafia" at ITV thought sending The Doc and his underling off to be with Northern Ireland meant that we were out of their way. I didn't mind. My role was to be a reporter and I was delighted.

Northern Ireland had qualified against the odds and were off to the finals for the first time since 1958. Their manager was Billy Bingham, who I knew well from his days at Everton. I'd interviewed him a few times back then. I would be spending a lot more time with him now.

Billy had the difficult task of trying to stay in the tournament as long as possible. Nobody gave them any hope. Just days before the first game, on the ITV preview show, both Ian St. John and Brian Clough scoffed at their chances.

They would eat their words later.

Northern Ireland had some real quality in the group. And a lot of mental toughness. Pat Jennings and Martin O'Neill being prime examples. There was also a young lad from Belfast; Norman Whiteside.

It seems daft describing Norman as a lad, he looked like a man despite turning only seventeen in May. He'd already made his debut for Manchester United. Now he was ready to take on the world.

Billy was brilliant with the players and they enjoyed his management style. I'd already won him over by telling him how I remembered him scoring against Cardiff in my first Everton game back in 1962.

Before setting off for Spain, Billy took the squad to Brighton for a training camp. He explained that the weather would be similar to Spain. When they got there, it was more than 25 degrees. Blue skies and a bright sun greeted us. It felt really warm. The sun left most of us squinting.

The boss had a solution.

Billy called the lads together and opened a suitcase. It was full of sunglasses.

"Lads, it's gunna be hot and sunny in Spain. Just like 'ere in Brighton. I've got these sunglasses 'ere for yoo to buy. Got 'em at a good price as well. Yoo're gunna need 'em".

The glasses weren't too expensive and he was bound to be selling them at cost price. The suitcase was emptied.

Later that day, we all went for a stroll along the seafront, slowly ambling along the promenade, not really paying attention to anything in particular. Then just like that, in front of us, outside a local souvenir shop we saw them.

A rack full of them.

The same sunglasses that Billy had sold to the players. And they were a lot cheaper too!!

Billy was the lowest paid manager going to the tournament. So he was always looking to make some extra cash. The lads christened him "FIFA". As in "fee for this" and "fee for that". Knowing Billy would accept money easily, we used it to our advantage to get as much access as possible. The Doc would give him a few pesetas for interviews.

When we got to Spain, I headed for Valencia. There was a famous ceramics factory, you've probably heard of called "Lladro". I visited it to do a small piece. While I was doing my report, I approached one of the ladies, who was working on a piece. I decided to try out my Spanish, so I could tell her that I appreciated what she was creating. Looking at a lovely vase, I said "muy bonita", which means very beautiful. I didn't think any more about it.

Back in Madrid, where ITV were based, someone decided that I was being a smart arse and trying to pull the woman in the factory! They thought I was telling her she was beautiful, not her work. I got my ear chewed about it. I was livid but I couldn't do anything about it.

I wasn't the only one covering Northern Ireland. The lads from Ulster TV were there too. Jackie Fullerton was the on-air reporter and he was brilliant. He was charismatic, passionate and well-known by the squad. The players trusted him and they liked being around him when the cameras stopped rolling. So did I. Jackie was a natural entertainer.

Jackie and I would be back together four years later for the next World Cup in Mexico. Don't worry, he continued to us entertain then too. Although it nearly got us in some serious trouble. I'll tell you about that in a bit.

I was particularly friendly with Northern Ireland physio Jimmy McGregor. He'd been at Everton and was now at Manchester United. Jimmy was great company.

Remember when Alex Ferguson used to chew a load of gum during games? That was Jimmy's idea. He told his boss that it would help with the stress.

Being mates with Jimmy helped me from the start because it gave me credibility with the players. If you're a friend of Jimmy's then you're bound to be alright.

During the tournament, I went out with Jimmy for a few. Terry Venables, who was scouting with England, joined us. Terry knew his stuff and was an interesting bloke. He also liked the limelight and enjoyed a singsong or two! His laugh was infectious and we had a good night.

As we got on extremely well, I was very surprised later in the decade when Terry refused to do a live match. When ITV asked him to be the guest, he said no. He explained it was because "Elton Welsby doesn't like me".

That wasn't true, I liked Terry. I don't know where that came from. There'd been no issue between us at all. Was it just an excuse not to do it? He'd worked with the BBC before. Was he being loyal to them? Who knows?

Okay, back to Spain.

Jimmy McGregor was concerned about the high temperatures and had a solution. He asked me to be behind the goal and throw water pouches to the lads. So I got in position and when necessary, threw on some water. Pat Jennings was always on hand to retrieve one. In fact, when the ball was up the other end of the field, Pat would have a chat with me.

There was also an overhead camera, which was above the pitch. Each time Pat had the ball, he would aim his kicks at the camera. When he failed to make contact, he turned to me.

"Missed again."

Then he got on with the game. Pat did this a few times. He never did hit that camera.

The Doc had us running around all the various training camps in Northern Ireland's group to get footage. Most of it was never used but no one could accuse us of being on a jolly.

We even tried Brazil's HQ, which was a nightmare. They trained behind closed doors and the closest we could get was on the wrong side of a tall wire-mesh fence. The Press Corp were shouting questions and the odd Brazilian player answered...briefly.

I found myself yards from Zico, who was the Pele of his day. Through the fence I gestured to him to take off his training top and throw it over to me.

He did.

Then I realised I needed proof. So I tossed it back and stuck a pen through the fence so he could autograph it.

He did.

That shirt was in the family for years until it'd been washed so often Zico's autograph had faded to nothing. Both my kids took turns to wear it.

Northern Ireland's 1982 adventure saw them qualify for the second phase after they memorably beat hosts Spain 1-0. When they were knocked out I was disappointed but proud of their achievements.

I went to ITV's quarters in Madrid after the Irish lads had gone home. I felt like a man out of place. They were obviously thinking "Doherty's boy is here. Let's give him something difficult to do and get rid of him for a bit".

"Go into the city and find someone famous to interview."

That was it.

I set off with a camera crew to a five-star hotel in the hope of meeting "someone famous".

Bingo!

The first person I recognised was the actor Roger Moore. As always he looked immaculate. He also had a lovely looking lady on his arm. I approached him with a cameraman and asked for a few words.

"My dear chap, I would absolutely love to and under the normal circumstances I would. But as you can see, I'm not alone. And she's not my wife."

James Bond bit the dust.

I didn't give up. I saw the concierge, who looked rather interested in why there was a camera crew in the hotel.

"Elton Welsby, ITV Sport from England. I'm looking for someone to speak to about the World Cup."

He didn't throw us out. Instead he helped.

"There IS someone of importance. Henry Kissinger."

This exceeded all my expectations.

"You need to clear it with his Secret Service team."

So I did. I sat in the reception with the camera crew waiting for an answer.

"Mr Secretary will do the interview with you now."

I had no idea where we were going do it. I asked the concierge, who found a room off the main reception area. We put two chairs in the room, facing each other.

"How do I actually address him?"

"Well, you call him Mr Secretary."

At this point he wasn't. But in the US, there are two political titles that you keep for life. One is the President and the other is the Secretary of State.

So Mr Secretary it was.

Kissinger came down and the level of security was unbelievable. He must've had Secret Service guys all around him. They had their little earpieces in. It was like a Hollywood film.

Henry Kissinger made it clear from the outset that under no circumstances do we speak about politics. That was fine by me. I only wanted to discuss football.

A security officer stepped in.

"You have three minutes Mr. Secretary."

We spoke for about fifteen. Kissinger was fantastic.

We were talking about one of his major passions in life. He was happy to keep going. I don't know how often he got the opportunity to do something like this. It certainly made a change from world peace.

I honestly don't think many people realised that Kissinger was such a huge fan of football. He adored the Hungary side of the 1950s and loved talking about them.

Henry Kissinger was born in Germany and was a supporter of his local side SpVgg Greuther Fürth. He always promised to go to a game if they were promoted to the Bundesliga.

In 2012, he got his wish.

He lived to the ripe old age of 100, passing away in 2023.

Once the interview was over, I returned to our HQ in Spain. They'd no idea where I'd been and who I'd been with. I don't think any of them were expecting me to come back with anything. I walked in and I was really pissed off with them.

I threw the tape on the table.

"Here you are. You wanted someone famous. You've got one. Henry Kissinger. Second most powerful man in the western world. Is that good enough?"

I was ready for home.

13

Bob and Brian

On 24th August 1982, the Shankly Gates were officially unveiled at Anfield. Just two days later, Bob Paisley announced that he'd be stepping down at the end of that season. Unlike Bill, who told the world after the 1974 FA Cup final win over Newcastle, Bob got the news out there nice and early.

The 1982/83 campaign would be his farewell tour.

We couldn't let Bob's retirement pass without a tribute to him. The Doc announced that we'd do a special show to honour the moment after the last game. The Doc also wanted someone from within football to present it.

He picked the perfect person.

Brian Clough.

Cloughie never got the England job. He should have. He deserved it. The suits at the FA were afraid of him. Like the people at ITV who feared The Doc, the FA were scared of Cloughie. I'm certain he would have been a huge success. But by his own admission, he'd have tried to take over the FA!

On the road to winning their first European Cup, Forest knocked out Liverpool in the first round. Liverpool were holders too. Cloughie had got one over Bob again just months after the League Cup win. At Granada TV, we ended up with a delicate situation. One of my colleagues ended up in the shit through no fault of his own.

No-one at Anfield would comment on the Forest defeat but we had to cover the story on Kick Off. It was huge. Two English teams meeting in the first round. The reigning champions Liverpool being knocked-out by Clough's side. One of the team, Richard Signy, came up with the idea that we close the show with a musical montage of the game's highlights. We had to use still photos as it was a BBC game so we had no access to the action.

Someone asked what music to use and quick as a flash, "Siggers" came up with "The Party's Over" by Frank Sinatra. The Doc agreed instantly.

By pure chance, Gerald Sinstadt did the final link. It could easily have been me but we alternated throughout the show and it was his turn. The reaction from the red side of Merseyside was incredible. And they didn't let Gerald forget it either. Poor old Gerry was hated at Anfield from that day on. It could easily have been me. I opened the show, he closed it. It was just pure luck.

It got nasty.

From then on when Granada were at Anfield, The Kop sang:

"Gerald Sinstadt, Gerald Sinstadt.
How's the party going now?"

When I went to Anfield, I'd just saunter in and be greeted with a "Alright Elt? how's it going la?" Little did they know. The Party's Over incident was a narrow escape and never again do I want to hear that fucking song!

With regards to the Bob Paisley tribute, all Cloughie had to do is agree to present it. I jumped the gun.

I was at Anfield for Liverpool versus Nottingham Forest in September 1982. It was a thrilling match, where Liverpool came from 3-2 down to win 4-3 with two late goals. I'd finished working and decided to enjoy a couple of drinks.

It was Dutch courage for what I was about to do; confront Cloughie for the first time.

"Hello Mr Clough, Elton Welsby, Granada TV."

"I know who YOU are."

I told him about the Bob Paisley programme and explained that we wanted him to present it. I was doing my best to sell it to him.

He cut me off.

"I'm a football manager. You're THE presenter."

"You, you do your job very well."

"I do my job even better."

"I wouldn't ask you to do my job."

"In fact, you can't do my job. I can't do your job. You're the presenter. Not me."

"I'LL DO IT!"

Then off he went.

My first ever conversation with Brian Clough didn't disappoint. The ice between us had been broken. Good job really, as I would work with him numerous times in the future. Even if I did have to be on my toes because of his unpredictable nature and comments. Cloughie would've been delighted that he was first choice. He loved the limelight. I allowed myself another drink to celebrate. Then I phoned The Doc.

On the field, Liverpool didn't suffer from the news of Bob's retirement and they won the title comfortably that season. They also won the League Cup for the third successive year. Now it was time for us to do the show.

The programme started brilliantly. Opening with a clip of Bob being worshipped by the Liverpool supporters, the scene switched to a deserted Anfield.

Brian Clough walked out of the tunnel and began proceedings:

"This place is going to seem a lot emptier now that Bob's decided to call it a day."

"But I'm not here to tell you how sorry I am that he's gone."

He paused momentarily.

"Frankly, we're GLAD to see the back of him!"

It was vintage Cloughie.

Brian then took us to the trophy room, highlighting exactly how successful Bob had been. Afterwards it was the famous boot room, where Roy Evans and Ronnie Moran were waiting for him. The rest of the show was mainly old interviews and clips of games. Cloughie reappeared at different points to add a bit of garnish to it all.

Everyone was happy with the tribute show and it stayed in the Granada archives. But it nearly came back to bite us much later on.

Bob Paisley's time as Liverpool manager had exceeded all expectations. Replacing Bill Shankly was an unenviable task, but Bob did it, taking the club to further glory. He was the man I called "Boss" and he was a lovely bloke. Like Shanks, I have so many fond memories of Bob.

Our final interaction was one of great sadness though.

Around 1994 I was at Anfield for a game. It was nice to catch up with some old faces. Friends and acquaintances. I was in the hospitality part when I saw Peter Robinson. He asked me to join him in another room. This was more than the VIP section. This was the heart of Anfield. As I walked through the door, I saw Bob Paisley sitting there. I hadn't seen him for a long time.

I went over to him immediately and shook his hand.

"Alright boss, how are you?"

Bob looked at me. He had no idea who I was.

I moved on and when the moment was right, I told Peter Robinson what had happened. He explained that Bob was suffering with his health and had dementia. Everything made sense. He looked totally lost when I greeted him.

That was the very last time I saw him.

Bob Paisley died in February 1996. Liverpool mourned another of its legendary managers.

I was working back at Granada when Bob passed away. My boss by then was a man called Paul McDowell. His claim to fame was that he'd presented the BBC show Newsround when John Craven wasn't available. He was no Paul Doherty. To say we didn't see eye to eye is an understatement. I didn't rate him at all. But I saved him from turning the red side of Liverpool against him and the station.

To pay tribute to Bob, McDowell had the brainwave of showing the retirement documentary from 1983 again. It was a ridiculous idea. Remember what Cloughie said at the start of that programme when talking about Bob retiring?

"I'm not here to tell you how sorry I am that he's gone. Frankly, we're glad to see the back of him!"

McDowell was clueless and was going to do it. I was furious. I went to the bar at Granada Studios, I needed a drink.

I had to try and think of how I could intervene. By luck, Wayne Garvie was already there. Wayne was director of broadcasting at Granada at this point, having started as a researcher in the sports department.

You'll hear more about Wayne later. He was another of Doc's finds. I told him what McDowell was planning to do. Wayne turned white. Before I could say anything else, he took off like a shot.

The programme never aired.

Instead, my colleague Don Jones and I worked on a fitting tribute to Bob, which was screened the night of his funeral.

McDowell didn't last long after that. I had lunch with the head of local programming Jeff Anderson. He asked me about McDowell. I told Jeff that McDowell was the most incompetent man I'd ever worked with or for.

After Bob's passing, we reached out to Nessie Shankly.

She thought she was going to be interviewed on "This Morning" and not just Granada. I was sat with her and explained what we were doing. I put her at ease.

We chatted mainly about Bob Paisley. But I couldn't resist. Naturally the conversation turned to her late husband Bill.

"What was Bill like when he got home after Liverpool lost?"

Without hesitation, she replied with a classic.

"I always knew, love. I didn't have to ask. He just used to come in and clean the oven."

I don't know if Nessie Shankly did any other interview during her whole life. That might've been her only one. She died in 2002, twenty-one years after her Bill.

14

Bowled Over

Although most people reading this know me because of football, I did other sports too.

You know by now how important The Doc was for my career. I've already mentioned that he was an innovator and would see things that others couldn't. The Doc was always looking for different projects to begin.

But one day, a few of us thought he'd lost his mind. His brainwave was to cover a sport that none of us knew anything about. One that we didn't think would be interesting for the viewers.

Doc's idea?

Bowls.

I can openly admit when this all began in the early 1980s, I knew nothing about the sport. It wasn't going to be plain sailing either. There were some hairy moments live on air. Also, behind the scenes, one man was plotting to reduce my responsibilities at Granada. A man looking for any reason to get me off the telly. I'll get to him later.

In 1982, bowls on Granada began; the Bass Masters live from Woodland Hotel, Ellesmere Port. And it led to one of my most uncomfortable moments on television.

On the first morning, I was interviewing bowler Bernard Marrow live on air. I was still pretty clueless about bowls. But I was doing okay for my first time. Bernard was a true Lancashire man, and you had to be from the Granada region to understand him.

Ursula Coburn was the production assistant. It was her job was to make sure that the programme started and finished on time. Ursula told me that I had only twenty seconds to fill. Then the credits would roll.

I asked Bernard a question about the competition. His reply was pure Lancastrian.

"Th'appen."

So I ended the interview.

"Thanks Bernard, and good luck in the second round."

Now I could sign off and finish.

Except Ursula got it wrong. The next thing she said really dropped me in the shit.

"Two minutes to credits."

What????

I was stumped and had to improvise quickly. I had to keep a serious face, while inside my mind was racing. You try speaking for two minutes into a camera about a subject that you barely know about.

It felt like a lifetime.

To make it even harder, in my earpiece I could hear a commotion. The Doc wasn't happy that I'd been dropped in it and was making his feelings known to Ursula. He was just a total pro and wouldn't accept shoddy work and low standards from anyone.

It was complete chaos and this was all going on in my ear as I tried to stay calm and talk about bowls. Miraculously I got there in the end. I probably said the same thing in ten different ways. As the programme ended and the cameras stopped rolling, I saw someone heading towards me.

It was one of the stagehands. He passed me a large whisky.

"I don't know how you did it, but you deserve this."

I didn't disagree. I necked it in one. At that point, I had no idea that I would fall in love with bowls.

A lot of people came to watch at the Woodland Hotel during that first tournament in 1982. Thanks to some nice weather and the momentum of the TV show, the place was full for the closing stages. It looked good for the viewers at home too. A packed house gave bowls credibility.

The Bass Masters became such a big event. It replaced the Waterloo bowling championships as the Holy Grail for bowlers. The Waterloo, from Blackpool, was like the FA Cup. But it couldn't match the Masters.

Inspired by what they saw on the screens and the chance to win some cash, the number of new bowlers increased by around 200%. In 1983, the prize money was £10,000 with £7,500 of it going to the winner. That's about £25,000 today. It was the biggest ever amount of prize money for a winner.

You can understand why people got the bug for bowls.

David Plowright was the managing director at Granada and he loved the whole experience of the Bass Masters. He had no problem agreeing to show more bowls. Paul had created this competition especially for television and it ran for 14 years. It was a new ingredient of daytime TV.

We added another tournament called the Greenall County Classic. It ran for six years and was made specially for television. It only stopped because the sponsor pulled out. At this time, bowls was covered primarily by Granada, with Yorkshire and Tyne Tees also dipping in a bit too. Then as its success grew, the interest did as well. It was time to get the sport on air nationwide.

Ambitious? Maybe. The decision was made to create yet another event. This one would open up bowls for national TV. Superbowl was born. But lurking in the background was someone with a grudge. And he was about to strike.

Mike Scott.

Scott's disdain for me started pretty early on. I hadn't been at Granada very long when The Doc asked me to attend a board meeting in 1978. I had no idea why, but I was new. I did as I was told. I still hadn't been on air yet.

In that board meeting was Mike Scott. He was climbing the ladder at the company and was on his way to becoming the programme controller. I don't know why, but he took an instant dislike to me. Being in that meeting felt like I was having an interview for a job I'd already got. It wasn't a nice experience.

Afterwards, I heard that Scott said a few things about me behind my back. He even asked someone if I was wearing a wig!! I wasn't even thirty. Of course I wasn't. Scott didn't just have a problem with me and my hairstyle. He didn't like The Doc either. He also hated sport.

From the moment he got promoted to his new position in 1979, he looked at how he could reduce the amount of coverage of sport on Granada. It was a stupid idea and a selfish one too. By the early 1980s, he managed to get rid of one of the most popular shows; Kick Off.

What was he thinking?

It was the perfect lead in to the weekend's fixtures, and with so many clubs in the area, we catered for their fans. We gave airtime to all the clubs, from Manchester United to Rochdale. Scott didn't give a shit about any of that. He used his personal feelings to make a decision that wasn't in the best interest of Granada TV. He was so political, but taking on The Doc was a mistake.

I don't even know if Scott watched Superbowl. Perhaps he made the decision out of spite. After the first programme aired, Scott told The Doc that I had to be removed from my presenting role immediately. There was no reason for it.

There was no way that Paul Doherty was going to let Scott win though. Incredibly, despite working there for years,

The Doc didn't have a contract with Granada. He went over Scott's head and straight to Plowright, and gave him an ultimatum.

Either I stayed as host of the bowls, or Paul would quit.

I couldn't believe that The Doc would do this. It was incredible. He took on Mike Scott, and defended me at the same time. Plowright had originally agreed with Scott but now he had a problem that he hadn't anticipated.

I'd already missed one show, being replaced as presenter by two commentators. It was car crash TV. It was terrible. They were good at their jobs but they weren't comfortable presenting. And it showed. They were out of their comfort zone. And their depth.

Plowright couldn't lose Paul. The Doc knew it too. Plowright gave in and told The Doc to do what he thought was right. So I kept the gig and was reinstated as the presenter.

That pissed Scott off even more.

Not only was I going to continue doing the bowls, but Paul had bypassed him to go to Plowright. It also fuelled the rivalry between Scott and Doc too. The Doc had shown Scott the contempt that he deserved.

David Plowright was THE major influence at Granada. His sister Joan was a famous actress and married to Sir Laurence Olivier. David organised a lavish big budget version of King Lear, to be shown on ITV. There was a strong cast and they were often milling around when I was at the studios.

One day, before I went on air, I was sat in the makeup chair. Next to me was this man with a long beard. He was explaining to another actor how he wanted to change the script. I couldn't believe it. This was a play written by William Shakespeare. What was going on?

After the man had left, I said to my makeup girl.

"You don't change fucking Shakespeare. Who does he think he is?"

"He's Sir Laurence Olivier."

Pity there were no selfies in those days!

After getting me back on Superbowl, The Doc felt he owed Plowright a favour. Plowright probably thought so too. So when he came to The Doc with an idea for another live event, Paul went against his better judgement.

Plowright was terribly posh and one of his favourite pastimes was croquet. He thought it'd be a good idea for Granada to cover it.

It was a ludicrous idea. The Granada region wasn't really a hotbed for croquet.

Who the fuck played croquet in Manchester or Liverpool?

But Doc owed him.

ITV's legendary horse racing commentator Lord John Oaksey was drafted in to work with me. He was considered a lot posher than me!

We were stationed under a canopy behind a trestle table. Underneath it at John's end were a couple of bottles of red wine. He started knocking back the claret once the games got underway. When The Doc realised, he went ballistic.

During a break, Doc approached Oaksey and made it clear how he felt about John's behaviour.

"Listen here, I don't give a fuck who you are, you don't get pissed when you're doing one of my shows, do you understand me???"

Doc was raging and Oaksey didn't know what to say or do. Having come from a privileged upbringing, I doubt he'd ever been spoken to like that before.

Doc was right though. He'd done the croquet to please Plowright. Now one of the people who was supposed to add a touch of class to the presentation was on the sauce. Like a good boy, I didn't touch a drop. As a rule, I only drank red wine with Tommy Cooper anyway!

Back to bowls. I have to admit, it was some of the most fun that I ever had working on TV. That might seem odd, but it was just brilliant. The people were really friendly. Those involved were delighted about the exposure that bowls was getting. It was attracting a respectable audience.

I was lucky enough to work with Hugh Johns too. Hugh was known for his football commentary in the Midlands and his trademark "one nothing" line. He was ideal for the bowls and I enjoyed spending time with him. He was another master of his trade. When I watch old matches with Hugh on commentary, I realise that it's a dying art.

The success of the bowls was unbelievable. In a bizarre turn of events, in her newspaper column, Janet Street-Porter wrote about how much she enjoyed Superbowl.

"It's presented in a very pally way," she wrote.

Very surreal.

15

The Renaissance

In 1983, Liverpool were still top dogs. Joe Fagan had slipped into Bob Paisley's shoes and they were carrying on where they left off.

Joe was another that I knew well from my Radio City days. I'd travelled around Europe with him in the 1970s as you know. I liked him. He was continuing the same traditions as Bob had done. All from the foundations that Bill Shankly built. Joe wasn't appointed until July, having been reluctant to follow Bob. Finally, he agreed to do it.

At Goodison Park though, there wasn't a golden sky. The clouds above were a lot darker. On 6th November, the Merseyside derby had finished with a one-sided 3-0 win for Liverpool at Anfield. It was painful. Everton were now managed by Howard Kendall. The legend. One-third of the Holy Trinity. A hero of mine. A man under pressure.

Despite his legacy as a player, the supporters were frustrated. They were voting with their feet. Attendances were down. Deep down nobody really wanted to turn against Howard, but with our neighbours showing no signs of giving up their domination, the heat was on. The fans were getting restless.

It's ironic that Howard replaced Gordon Lee. When Gordon was still the boss, Mick Lyons had a testimonial pitting Everton's present team against a side of former Toffees. The ex-players might've been a little older than the current lot but there was some serious talent on show.

I was fortunate enough to be sat on the bench. Gordon was really taken by one of the lads, who stood out more than the rest.

So he asked Colin Harvey, who was next to him.

"Err...Col, who's that there? He's great. Fuckin' hell Col. He's really got it. Who is it?"

"Howard Kendall, boss."

How could Gordon not recognise Howard Kendall?

Not long after the Anfield humiliation in November 1983, I headed off to Goodison for Granada Reports. I was there to record a piece in advance of the Milk Cup tie with Coventry City. A home draw was welcome, but nobody was truly confident of a win. Pessimism was rife.

When I met up with Howard, he looked tired. The stress was getting to him. After the loss at the weekend, we were down in 17th place. Four league wins from twelve games wasn't good enough. Nobody knew that more than Howard.

We did a bog standard piece for Granada, nothing out of the ordinary. We finished and I started to pack my things away. The cameraman did the same and went, leaving me alone with Howard.

"Elt, can we have a chat please? You know, as two Evertonians together. Not for TV purposes."

"Of course, no problem."

"We're struggling. I know I can make this work. I want to know what you think. You're a fan. What do the supporters want?"

"Well H. I think I speak for most of us when I say that we want to see winning, entertaining football."

"I'm going to make some changes. I'm going to promote Colin Harvey to be my assistant. He'll be alongside me."

Colin had been working as a coach at the club for a bit. Howard wanted someone next to him that he could trust. Someone he was certain he could rely on. They'd been magic together on the field. Now it was time for them to rediscover their golden touch to save the season. Probably Howard's job too.

Then H told me something else. He was dipping into the transfer market. Howard had already brought in players like Neville Southall, Peter Reid and Trevor Steven since his arrival. Now he felt he just needed one last piece of the jigsaw to make the difference.

"We're going to sign Andy Gray. He's what we need to give the dressing room a bit more bite."

For those of you who only know Andy for his TV work, I can tell you that he was some player. He burst on the scene at Dundee United before arriving at Aston Villa. He then had a big money move to Wolverhampton Wanderers. But Wolves were having some financial problems and a fee for Andy would help them.

There were doubts about Andy's fitness though.

"He's got a problem with his knee. I reckon he'll fail his medical. I just need to convince the chairman Phillip Carter that he'll be fine."

Andy Gray wasn't just a top striker. There was more to him than that. And Howard knew Andy's qualities.

"He's for the dressing room. We need him in there. Even if he hardly plays. I need as many leaders as possible."

Howard didn't see it as a gamble. Besides, he was running out of cards to play. I was excited by the thought of Andy joining. Howard hadn't finished yet either.

"Peter Reid will play some part against Coventry too. He'll be in centre midfield. That's his true position."

Reidy had suffered from injuries, even before he came to Goodison. Howard was true to his word. Reidy came off the bench to play in the heart of midfield.

"This stays between you and me, Elt. OK? I don't want this getting out."

I was chuffed that he trusted me.

I had three major scoops before the cup match but couldn't use any of them. But I didn't care. I'd been in this situation before, especially with Bob Paisley. I had no intention of ruining my relationship with Howard.

When kick-off arrived for the Coventry game, there was still a lot of doom and gloom around the ground. Only 9,000 turned up. It was a dreadful number. You could hear the players communicating with each other. Colin Harvey was on the bench with Howard, just as H had said he'd be.

The match wasn't pretty.

When Dave Bamber put the Sky Blues ahead, a cup exit was on the cards. An equaliser from Adrian Heath in the 79th minute kept our hopes alive. Then Graeme Sharp popped up with a 90th minute winner to send us through.

The 2-1 win was welcome, even if it was nerve-wracking stuff. The tide turned when Peter Reid came on as sub. As Howard foretold, he played in centre midfield.

Then Andy Gray signed.

Many people believe that the turning point in Everton's fortunes came two months later. In the Milk Cup quarter-final away to Third Division Oxford United. A late Heath goal forced a replay. It all came from a bad back pass from Oxford's Kevin Brock.

I don't think that was the moment.

I truly believe that having Colin on the bench with Howard was massive. The two of them knew each other so well. Howard had an ally with him. Add the signing of Andy to that, plus Reidy's new role. These three factors together were the catalyst for the upturn.

We became harder to beat and slowly started to climb the table. And progress was being made in the two domestic cups. Peter Reid and Andy Gray were extra leaders to compliment the ones we already had, like skipper Kevin Ratcliffe.

Oxford were beaten in the replay and then a 2-1 aggregate victory over Aston Villa saw Everton going to Wembley for the Milk Cup final. At the same time, the FA Cup was still a possibility. Morale was a lot higher.

It was no coincidence for me that it was since Andy Gray had become part of the squad. Andy was a warrior. He put his head where the boots were flying. His courage and leadership were infectious.

Eventually we had an FA Cup semi-final to look forward to in April. That would be at Highbury against Southampton. The other semi? At Villa Park, Watford against Third Division Plymouth Argyle, who were enjoying a fairytale cup run.

Now all eyes were looking towards Wembley Stadium. The Milk Cup final 1984. Everton versus Liverpool.

But just a few days before that, there was a big European game in Manchester. Trailing 2-0 from the first leg, United had a mountain climb in their European Cup Winners' Cup quarter-final against Barcelona. It wasn't even live on TV either. The viewers at home had to settle for highlights.

I'd checked into my hotel in Manchester about tea time. I changed in the room and got the lift down to the ground floor.

I wasn't alone.

Sharing the ride was Diego Armando Maradona.

We shook hands and that was about it. He didn't speak a word of English. I suppose what struck me most was his height. Maradona was 5'4". I was looking down on him.

Within a few years I came to regard him as the greatest of all time, just ahead of Cruyff, Pelé and Best.

That night at Old Trafford has gone down as one of the most unforgettable in United's history. The fans who were there talk about it still. There must've been 200,000 in the ground that night if every one of them is telling the truth!

Bryan Robson was the hero, scoring twice. After the 3-0 win, there was a pitch invasion and Bryan was lifted shoulder high. He also kept Maradona quiet too.

I was waiting for Robbo as he came down the tunnel. After his manager Ron Atkinson hugged him, I grabbed a quick word. Then Big Ron himself, smiling from ear to ear, joined in. He said he was going to have a cup of tea to celebrate.

As Ron himself would say:

"Are you sure?"

There was just time to breathe before we went onto the first ever Merseyside derby at a domestic cup final. There would be more during this decade but this was the first. It seemed like a great opportunity for Granada to produce a documentary on the rivalry and what the city would be like in the build-up to the match.

It didn't work out as I wanted it to.

For some reason, the sports department collaborated with the news and current affairs team. It made no sense. Instead of an exciting piece to get everyone in the mood for the final, it looked at the darker side of the city. Although I didn't mind the interview in Walton jail between two rival fans. A Red and a Blue.

The 1980s were hard for the people of Liverpool, and this documentary certainly didn't paint it in a positive light. There wasn't enough stuff about the game. Too many people got involved and it was a depressing piece of television. It should've been so much more.

On the day of the final, I visited the hotel room of Kenny Dalglish and Graeme Souness. The two Scots arrived at Anfield within a few months of each other and were roommates for the big occasion.

It was telly gold.

Especially, when out of the blue, Arsenal striker and fellow Scotsman Charlie Nicholas appeared. We were filming everything, and it was clear that the footage would be remembered for years. The three of them were on great form.

None of it made air. I've no idea why.

Kenny and Graeme were walking around their room wearing just towels, perhaps someone felt it was a bit too much. The viewers missed out. I've no doubt it would've still been shared today online too. It was that good.

The final itself wasn't very exciting. It ended 0-0 and it meant that there would have to be a replay. Instead of it being at Wembley, common sense prevailed and the two teams met again at Maine Road. Souness scored the only goal and Joe Fagan had his first trophy as Liverpool boss. It wouldn't be his last either.

But he wouldn't be getting his hands on the FA Cup. Only one Merseyside club had a chance of that.

The final was between Everton and Watford.

Or Elton versus Elton, as my late colleague Bob Greaves said on Granada Reports.

Everton won 2-0 thanks to goals from Graeme Sharp and Andy Gray. It's no exaggeration to say that a weight had been lifted off of our shoulders. We'd waited far too long for this moment. Now it was time for Evertonians to celebrate.

Something was stirring at Goodison Park.

16

Saints alive

You've gathered by now that I'm an Evertonian. But from being a kid, I've another loyalty.

If you come from St. Helens, rugby league and the Saints are in your DNA. There are very few in the town who have no interest in the sport. But even they still ask: "How did the Saints get on?"

My first memory dates back to 1958. That's when I can first remember people talking about rugby league. We used to go to my Aunty Ethel and Uncle Bert's every Sunday. It'd always be a huge family gathering. There'd be a fair few of us. This one day, the adults were talking about one player in particular.

The thing that sticks out the most is what my Aunty Ethel said:

"Oh, he's a cocky little so and so."

They were talking about Alex Murphy.

From that moment onwards I became interested in the sport. And Alex Murphy would be an enormous reason for that.

So why were my aunties and uncles talking about him?

Great Britain had just travelled for a three-match series over in Australia. A place where they never seemed to win. After some travel problems hindered their arrival, it was no shock when the Aussies won comfortably in the first test.

Enter Alex Murphy.

After inspiring the team to a 25-18 victory to tie the series, Murphy was man of the match. He must've been brilliant to win the accolade. His captain Alan Prescott played on after breaking his arm in the opening minutes. Yet Alex took the plaudits.

Murphy was the hero once more when Great Britain beat the hosts 40-17 in the deciding game. The local lad had done it again. The British Lions came home with a series win. He was the talk of the town with a try in each of the two winning games.

Ray French is another local hero. He played both rugby union and league. In his book, Ray described Alex Murphy as the greatest rugby player he'd ever seen or played with. French included both codes, not just rugby league.

Ray tells the story about how he used to catch Alex combing his hair before leaving the dressing room.

"Hey Spud! Why are combing your hair? This is rugby league!"

"Frenchie, your mum and dad are coming to see you. 22,000 people are coming to see me."

Alex Murphy. Never short on confidence. Aunty Ethel was right.

One thing that helped Alex was that he had a minder. Vince Karalius, known as "The Wild Bull of the Pampas". It was like he was made of granite. Like Alex, he played for Saints and Great Britain.

During one game, Vince got the ball at the back of the scrum and sent Alex on his way. Murphy sidestepped a couple of challenges and headed for the line to score a try. Before he got there, Karalius shouted to him:

"Don't go under the sticks. You'll never get your head through!"

Karalius later became a head coach. Over at Widnes RLFC, Jim Mills was his chief enforcer for a part of Vince's spell. Big Jim, as he was known, was sent off a lot in his career.

I hosted a Manchester Evening News Sports Personality Awards ceremony at the Midland Hotel. I spotted Jim near the back of the room and announced he was there.

"Big Jim Mills, everyone, a giant of rugby league, sent off 17 times in his career."

Jim responded immediately.

"18!"

Jim had a nightclub in Widnes with teammate Kurt Sorensen. I went one night. The two of them wore tuxedos and wandered around the place, checking everything was okay. They looked more intimidating than Ronnie and Reggie. No wonder it was the most trouble-free club in Widnes, or anywhere else for that matter. We could've done with them at The Shakey!

As the years passed, Alex Murphy went from a great playing career to becoming a successful coach. And that's when our paths first crossed and our friendship began.

In 2006, I'd organised for Fred Trueman to speak at the local school where my kids used to go to. Fred had to pull out at the last minute with ill health. It was the day of the event. I called Alex, explained the situation and asked if he could step in. He didn't hesitate and did a cracking job. Sadly, Fred Trueman died a few days later.

As it was more popular in the north of England, rugby league was shown on Granada and Yorkshire in the 1980s. We showed highlights of the first half and then the second half would be live. Whenever possible, we picked a Lancashire versus Yorkshire match.

My studio companion was "The Wild Bull of the Pampas" himself; Vince "Vinty" Karalius. The excellent and underrated John Helm was the commentator.

One day we were at Headingley in Leeds. Jeff Hall was the director. He loved a glass or two of Scotch.

During the game!

Even though it was only in Leeds, we were staying overnight in a hotel. There was Vinty, Jeff and myself. We were in the lounge, chatting about the game when Jeff decided that he wanted to go to the casino downstairs. He was feeling lucky. Vinty and I didn't fancy it, so we stayed in the lounge.

About an hour had passed and Jeff hadn't come back. We thought it might be a good idea to check if he was alright. He wasn't. There were about three or four louts about to rough him up.

"Come on lads, no problem, let's just have a good night."

One of the group snarled at me.

"And what are YOU gonna do about it?"

"Me? Nothing."

I pointed over at Vinty.

"But he might."

After taking one look at "The Wild Bull of the Pampas", they scarpered.

The 1984/85 season is a personal favourite of mine. It became known as the Mal Meninga season, after the arrival of Australia's star player at Saints. Big Mal was regarded as best player in the world.

And he was at our club!

I did an interview for Granada Reports with Mal and the coach Billy Benyon at the club's Knowsley Road ground in the autumn of 1984. Billy then asked me if I could pop into the dressing room in the future, just to say hello to the lads.

I took our Chris with me to the next home match. When Billy saw me, he invited us in. As I wished them well and went to leave, Neil Holding, who was the joker in the side, couldn't resist.

"See you at half-time, coach!"

It became a ritual. Both Chris and I started sitting on the bench. We also had our places on the team bus too.

In truth, Meninga wasn't always fully fit. He was still imperious. There were times when he shouldn't have played but Billy convinced him to. Mal's presence alone was enough to intimidate the opposition.

The Lancashire Cup Final against Wigan was a big occasion. And made even more difficult because the venue was Central Park, Wigan's home ground.

In the dressing room beforehand, Billy nudged me.

"Can you have a word with Sean Day? He's shitting himself."

Sean was the left winger and a ball of nerves.

"Alright Sean, how are you doing?"

"Oh it's a big game, yer know."

"What have you got to fucking worry about? You've got the best player in the world inside you."

He was playing alongside Meninga, who was outside centre. And the thought of that was putting his mind at rest. Sean Day kicked five goals and scored a try in that final. Saints beat Wigan 26-18 on their own patch.

Things were really buzzing at Knowsley Road during Meninga's season.

But how would Saints do without him? I thought I had the answer.

Joe Lydon, who was a pal at the time, was ready to leave Widnes. I convinced Joe that he should join Saints and effectively replace Meninga at the end of the season. Joe was the reigning Man of Steel, rugby league's highest individual award.

Around Christmas time, Joe and I went along to Knowsley Road for a night game. After the match we met with coach Billy Benyon.

"Merry Christmas, Bill. Here's your present."

Billy was delighted.

He immediately went into the board room to meet the directors with the good news.

"Joe Lydon is here and he wants to commit to us for next season."

Basically, the board said no, they couldn't afford it.

It was such narrow-minded thinking. Mal was getting very well reimbursed for his year-long contract so surely it would be a case of Meninga out, Lydon in.

Joe went to Wigan at the end of the following season for a rugby league record of £100,000. But that was Saints' problem back then; they didn't think big enough. To rub salt in, over the next ten years Joe Lydon was a vital cog in one of the most successful club sides in the history of the game.

The Meninga season reached its pinnacle on 11th May 1985 at Elland Road in Leeds. Saints' victory over Hull Kingston Rovers saw the club crowned Premiership champions. It was a wonderful day in the history of the club. There was a picture of Chris and I in the St. Helens Star, fist punching for Maninga, as he went in for the all-important try.

I'll jump forward now because I've one more personal story to share.

In 1995, the Bosman ruling became law in football. Inevitably it would apply to rugby league as well. My cousin Bill asked me if I could act as an agent for his lad, Mark, whose contract was up for renewal at Swinton RLFC.

So the tactic I used in negotiations was that Mark would just walk away unless the club made him a far better offer. With Bosman looming, the general manager realised he was powerless to keep Mark if we weren't satisfied with the terms.

He didn't have a leg to stand on. Mark got what he wanted and deserved.

17

If I can dream

The 1984/85 season began with the traditional Wembley Charity Shield match between league champions and FA Cup winners. This meant another Merseyside derby under the shadows of the Twin Towers. It was a baking hot day and after an odd own goal from Liverpool keeper Bruce Grobbelaar, Everton won 1-0.

After a dodgy start to the league season, things began to improve, including a 5-0 battering of Manchester United. The scoreline made people sit up and take notice.

I was also celebrating. My daughter Laura was born on 20th September. I had one of each now!

At Christmas, Spurs were top of the league, followed by Manchester United. Everton sat in third, just two points behind Tottenham. In Europe, there were wins over Inter Bratislava and Fortuna Sittard. The excitement was tempered a little, however, when Everton were drawn to face Bayern Munich. The West Germans were a superpower in Europe and had a fearsome reputation.

A 0-0 draw in Munich was positive but with away goals always a clear and present danger, we were right to be a little anxious about the second leg. As league leaders, it was time to face the challenge of Bayern Munich on home soil. This was going to be a huge test.

What happened against Bayern is still talked about today. It remains one of the best nights in the history of Goodison Park. It wasn't live on television but I was there covering the match. The highlights were shown later that night.

With the score at 0-0 and half-time on the horizon, Bayern dealt a hammer blow to Everton's hopes. Dieter Hoeness put the visitors in front. Everton would need two goals to get through now. Nerves were jangling. Howard Kendall had a big team talk to give during the break.

Whatever happened in that dressing room had an instant impact. Graeme Sharp made it 1-1 within three minutes.

In the 73rd minute, Everton took the lead. It had to be Andy Gray. The player signed by Howard, his final roll of the dice back in 1983, had stepped up again. Bayern were still dangerous though and pushed on looking to level the tie, which would see them go through. They had to leave gaps. Everton exploited them. With only four minutes to go, Trevor Steven made it 3-1.

Bayern were on their knees.

Everton were in the final!

Goodison was rocking. My mind went back to Liverpool's dramatic night against St. Etienne in 1977. I remember thinking we'd matched the greatest European night in their history. I didn't have too long to think though, I had to get to work.

I ran to our camera position downstairs. First up the tunnel was Andy, who made a beeline towards me. We managed an interview together before I went to share a beer or two in celebration with the rest of the lads. The club had been struggling. Now it was on the verge of winning the league and had secured its place in a European final.

As the beer flowed, one of Howard's assistants Mick Heaton began to tell a story. The second half had been like blitzkrieg in reverse. Everton bombarded the Bayern rearguard for Sharp and Gray to rough 'em up.

At one point the Bayern coach Udo Lattek yelled over to the Everton bench. He was furious.

"Meester Kendall zis eez not football."

Howard replied:

"Fuck off!"

Everton were going to Rotterdam. That's all that mattered.

If anyone thought that being in the Cup Winners' Cup final would distract the players, they were wrong. Wins over Norwich and Sheffield Wednesday meant that Everton needed three points against QPR at Goodison Park on 6th May to lift the title.

I was covering the game for Thames Television on their Bank Holiday Monday show, positioned on the television gantry. Reporting though, not commentating.

I was doing my preview piece, which was meant to last about 15 seconds. Then I heard someone in my ear.

"Elton, there's a problem here. We can only get you. Keep talking. Keep talking."

What problem? If anyone knew what to say at Goodison Park, it was me.

"And of course similar scenes to those in 1963, when Everton beat Fulham by four goals to one. Skipper Roy Vernon getting a hat trick.

And back in 1970, when Howard Kendall and Colin Harvey played in that fantastic midfield which included Alan Ball. They beat West Brom 2-0 that day, with Colin Harvey scoring the second."

Personal memories, used in a professional way.

The result was never in doubt. A 2-0 victory was enough. After waiting fifteen years, Everton were finally champions once more. The fact that both Howard and Colin were involved wasn't lost on me. Getting over the line early meant that the players could relax before going to Holland for the final against Rapid Vienna. The two league games beforehand were irrelevant. Everything was focused on trying to win another trophy.

It was to be live on ITV. The Doc headed up a Granada team in Rotterdam. Brian Moore and Cloughie would provide the commentary. On the morning of the match, Duncan McKenzie and I went for a stroll around the city. We saw what we initially thought was a mob of Everton fans. We feared the worst. But the Everton fans were playing football with the local police. Riot shields and batons marked out the pitch.

It was fantastic.

Two weeks later, there were very different scenes at the European Cup final, which rocked English football to its core.

Heysel.

UEFA were very strict about journalists getting access. They'd limited the number of people representing the different TV companies, radio stations and newspapers. Having the relationship that I did with the club meant that I was able to call in a favour or two. What happened next was crazy and certainly not possible today.

I was smuggled onto the bench as part of the Everton squad. Disguised as a substitute! Howard Kendall had agreed to it all. I had a microphone hidden inside my top.

During the game, Brian Moore was going to come to me and I'd interview John Bailey, who was an official sub. This happened twice in the first half and then twice in the second half. I couldn't hear Mooro. But The Doc signalled to me when it was time. Then I'd speak to Bails.

Everton won 3-1 that night. With my position so close to the action, I was able to get onto the pitch. Before Kevin Ratcliffe lifted the cup, I got round some of the players for snap interviews. I was like a pig in shit!

After the joy of wining two trophies in two weeks, Everton had only three days before another Wembley date. The Blues were overwhelming favourites against Manchester

United. The game wasn't pretty. Then came the dramatic moment. With just over ten minutes to go, Peter Reid intercepted a wayward pass from Paul McGrath and headed forward. Kevin Moran flew in and took Reidy down. It was a clear foul. It deserved a booking.

Ex-policeman Peter Willis was officiating his last ever game. He decided to grab the headlines. He sent Kevin off, making him the first player to receive his marching orders in a FA Cup final. Reidy pleaded with Willis to change his mind. That shows you all you need to know about Peter Reid. What a gesture that was.

The ten men of United held on and with the score locked at 0-0, the match went into extra-time. With ten minutes to go, Norman Whiteside scored an outstanding goal to win the cup for United. It had to be special; Neville Southall in Everton's goal was arguably the best keeper in Europe. If not the world.

The season still wasn't over yet.

There was still Wednesday 29th May.

Liverpool, the holders of the European Cup were in the final, attempting to retain the trophy. Juventus, a great side with players like Platini, Rossi and Boniek, looked a formidable opponent. The game was held at the Heysel Stadium in Brussels, Belgium. The ground, home to other big matches in the past, was decrepit.

It was a terrible choice of venue.

Fighting had broken out on the terraces. The TV cameras were rolling and we saw a lot of graphic images. A wall collapsed and people were crushed to death. It was horrific.

39 people died in total.

UEFA then made a ridiculous decision. The match took place. Who wanted to play? Who wanted to watch? Everyone was in shock. Platini scored a penalty and

Juventus won 1-0. It was Joe Fagan's last game as Liverpool boss. Poor Joe. It had a massive impact on him.

Europe's governing body came to the decision that enough was enough. All English clubs were now banned indefinitely from European club competitions.

18

What a result

World of Sport had been a staple of Saturday afternoons on ITV since 1965. Three years after it first aired, Dickie Davies became the presenter and was the face of the show. Until September 1985 that is, when the channel decided to cancel it.

One of the most successful parts of World of Sport was the results service, which started just before the final whistles blew at football matches up and down the country. Millions tuned in, some with their pools coupons in hand, seeing if they'd won big money.

Although World of Sport came to an end, there were still parts of it that kept going. The Saint and Greavsie show was born out of the "On the Ball" segment. The two ex-players had teamed up and their unique chemistry was a hit with viewers. ITV decided the duo could go it alone. It was a great success, very funny and is fondly remembered.

The results service was to continue. It was the highest rated bit of World of Sport. It became my job to present it. I'd already got the hang of it when covering Dickie a couple of times. The upside was that I'd get more exposure on network television. My future was looking bright.

I'd take a short flight from Manchester to London and then do the same for the way back. It was a popular route and you'd always bump into someone. One Saturday night, it was a megastar. Tony Bennett, the American singer was going to Manchester. He was at the front of the plane. I was only one seat behind him. I didn't realise it was him at first. There were only about 20 people on board. I stood up, back to the cockpit, and announced his presence. Bennett got up and bowed. All the passengers applauded.

I didn't leave it at that.

"Come on Mr. Bennett. I know the lyrics. All together now..."

Having had a few drinks, I broke into song!

"The loveliness of Paris, seems somehow sadly gay. The glory that was Rome is of another day."

Tony Bennett joined in and was a great sport. He appeared to enjoy it. After the duet, I sat next to him for 15 minutes or so and we were just nattering until the plane landed. It was such a crazy thing. It was a spur of the moment happening.

Luckily, I knew the words to I Left My Heart In San Francisco!

Kick Off might have been killed off, but Granada still covered local football. If a story broke, or there was a big game coming up, I was the man on the scene. In the 1980s and 1990s, the player/manager was all the rage. When Joe Fagan retired in 1985, Kenny Dalglish took over at Anfield. In that same year and just a few miles away, Tranmere Rovers also went down the same route.

They appointed Frank Worthington.

Remember that incredible goal Frank scored for Bolton Wanderers against Ipswich Town back in 1979? A goal so good that the referee was caught on camera applauding it. Jimmy Armfield and myself were at Burnden Park together. Neither of us could believe it.

Back to goal, Frank juggled the ball and flicked it over the head of Terry Butcher, before firing in on the volley. I swear there was a stunned split second of silence before the crowd erupted.

Frank Worthington was an exciting and skilful player. He was also known for enjoying himself off the field. We'd all heard stories about Frank. He was one of the game's mavericks. I couldn't see him as a manager though.

I went to Prenton Park with a camera crew. Frank didn't disappoint.

We arranged for the players to be outside the ground, to greet Frank and his assistant George Mulhall. We'd agreed they'd park up before driving through the gates so we could get it all set up with the players in shot.

Cue George, who was driving. In they came, with the players looking apprehensive. George parked the car and Frank got out. The players were flabbergasted. This was not acting. It was real.

Out of the car stepped their new manager wearing a Stetson hat, tight jeans, cowboy boots and a t-shirt with the following words across the front:

SHIT STINKS

"Welcome to Tranmere Rovers, boss!"

Frank did well and also scored a fair few goals. I didn't expect him to stay too long but he did. And he brought publicity to the club. At one away game at Exeter, he bumped into some Tranmere fans and bought them all a drink.

I'd also like to take this opportunity to dispel a rumour.

I'm not a Tranmere Rovers fan.

I've a soft spot for them as they're the closest professional club to where I live on The Wirral. It used to be a tradition that Tranmere played their home games on a Friday night. It was a convenient way to start a weekend of football. Managers and scouts from other clubs would go to Prenton Park on Friday nights. Whoever the visiting manager to Anfield or Goodison was that weekend, I'd normally see them at Tranmere. It meant I was able to keep in touch with many in the game.

Of course, I wanted Tranmere to do well but that used to apply to all the clubs in the Granada region.

The better for them, the better for us.

I had some great nights there when Johnny King was manager and then John Aldridge. With Aldo, of course, there was the South Liverpool connection. But it was nothing more than that. I only support Everton.

Goodison Park was the place to be during this era, after winning the FA Cup in 1984 and another two trophies in 1985. I could never have imagined that Kenny Dalglish as player/manager would turn out so well for Liverpool.

I should've known better.

During pre-season, Andy Gray departed for Aston Villa. I was extremely disappointed. Andy's record was impressive. He scored 22 goals in 66 appearances. His impact on the club was enormous. Andy was only 29 years old when he left. In my opinion, he had more to give us.

Andy didn't just score run-of-the-mill goals. He scored vital goals. Not a tap-in to make it 5-0. He lifted those around him. Howard Kendall knew what he was getting when he signed Andy. Howard probably got even more than he expected. The club paid £250,000 for Andy and sold him for £150,000. He certainly paid for himself. To this day, Andy still loves Everton.

Gary Lineker arrived from Leicester City to play alongside Graeme Sharp for the new season. His profile was totally different to Andy's. He was a pure goal scorer, mainly from inside the box. I don't know how much he added in terms of leadership in the dressing room. He couldn't take Andy's place in that regard.

Being a fixture on Saturday afternoon television was enjoyable. The ratings for the results service were excellent. We became known for being slightly ahead of the BBC with the latest scores and results. That certainly helped.

The season itself was strange. With no European football for English clubs, there was a real void in the calendar. As an Evertonian, I was left to reflect on what might have been.

When the first day arrived in August, there was still no TV deal in place. The Football League couldn't find an agreement with ITV or the BBC. Football was in the doldrums. Hooliganism had made it less attractive. Families didn't want to go to games. Attendances were going down.

With no contract agreed, so much footage was never shown in England. When there was a big match, you'd see overseas TV companies setting up to beam back the matches. But none of us could watch along. It was terrible.

Manchester United won their first ten games and were ten points clear at the top of the table. They were playing fast, exciting, attacking football under Big Ron. Neither ITV nor the BBC were showing any of it. Which meant there were no live games on Sunday afternoons either.

Finally, a contract was signed and in January 1986, football was back on the telly. By then United were wobbling and both Everton and Liverpool were taking them on for the league championship. Gary Lineker was scoring a hatful and Kenny Dalglish was carrying on the Anfield traditions he'd learnt from his predecessors.

By Easter, it was down to the two Merseyside clubs. It was the same in the FA Cup.

When Liverpool beat Chelsea at Stamford Bridge in early May, they were crowned champions. It was fitting that the only goal of the game came from Kenny. He picked himself and he scored the winner. The title was back at Anfield. If they could beat us in the final, they'd win the league and cup double for the first time in their history.

The FA Cup final was the hottest ticket in town and touts were asking for a small fortune. It got to the point where fans were scaling the side of Wembley to climb inside. It was crazy. My old mate Tom O'Connor described it as "Colditz in reverse".

Gary Lineker scored in the first half to put Everton ahead. I was sitting next to Greavsie, he tapped me on the knee and said: "Don't worry son, it's in the bag".

He was wrong. A comeback in the second half saw Liverpool win 3-1. Ian Rush, so often Everton's nemesis, got two. If only he'd signed for Manchester City back in the day!

Lineker's record that season was incredible. With thirty-eight goals overall, he finished top scorer in the country. That FA Cup final goal proved to be Lineker's last for the club. After the World Cup, he was off to Barcelona for £2.2 million. His arrival saw a change in style of play. I think Sharp and Gray worked better than Sharp and Lineker.

With domestic business over, all eyes turned to international football. I was assigned to go to another World Cup. They were sending me to Mexico to be with the Northern Ireland squad again. The Doc was going to be out there with me too.

Another major tournament. I couldn't wait!

19

Mexico 86

Four years on from Spain, I was back at another World Cup with Northern Ireland. We were off to Mexico!

We nearly weren't though.

In September 1985, a huge earthquake hit Mexico City. Over 5,000 people died and the cost of the damage was more £3 billion. Mexico wasn't the original choice either. Back in 1974, Colombia won the rights to host it. Colombia later backed out and Mexico was chosen.

The decision was controversial. Both Canada and the United States put forward their bids. When the result went in Mexico's favour, the other nations weren't happy. My "old pal" Henry Kissinger spoke up. He saw it as unfair and smelt corruption. Canada said that Mexico's proposal was "a joke".

Corruption in football? Surely not.

Now after the terrible disaster, Mexico's role was in doubt. But with none of the stadiums affected, the decision was made to continue with the preparations.

Before we arrived in the country, we visited the US first. Due to the high sea level in Mexico, it was important to do altitude training. This meant going to The Rockies. That produced a memorable piece of VT (video tape).

Shown on Saint and Greavsie, the clip was of Norman Whiteside and myself running together with the rest of the squad at the foothills of the mountains outside Albuquerque, New Mexico.

The scenery was breathtaking.

Pat Pearson edited the footage and the track played was "Up Where We Belong" by Joe Cocker and Jennifer Warnes. ITV head of sport John Bromley messaged us after transmission to say that was the best piece sent by any ITV team in the World Cup build-up.

I didn't realise but the choice of song was rather poignant for me. I'm going to steer us off course for a moment. "Up Where We Belong" was originally written and sung by Buffy Sainte-Marie. Many of you might not know of her.

In the early 1970s, despite having my job at the Liverpool Weekly News, I went into higher education. I studied at Harris College in Preston. I decided to write my thesis on the plight of the indigenous tribes of North America. I'd been inspired by the film Soldier Blue and wanted to know more.

The film covers the massacre at Sand Creek in Colorado, where the Cheyenne and Arapaho tribes were killed by the US Army in 1864. Women and children were butchered. The haunting music soundtrack featured Buffy Sainte-Marie. I was so moved by it that I contacted her record company. I wanted to talk to her about it.

They took a message and I left it at that. Within 24 hours, I received a call. It was Buffy Sainte-Marie. I couldn't believe it. She went into a lot of detail about Sand Creek and also another massacre, the one at Wounded Knee. We also discussed Little Big Horn, also renowned as Custer's Last Stand.

When I handed in my work, my tutor's reaction to my work was disappointing.

"Fascinating. This is all fiction though, isn't it?"

"IT'S NOT."

Now back to 1986 and The Rockies.

Looking back, whoever organised the preparation for Northern Ireland knew what they were doing. Arranging altitude training before going to Guadalajara was smart.

The lads were going to play their game at about 7,000 feet above sea level. They needed to adjust in advance.

Big Pat Jennings had seen nothing like it. The players were taking shots from distance and they were whistling over his head and into the net. It took Pat a couple of sessions to get used to it. There's a reason why so many long shots were attempted once the tournament began.

We were with the lads from Ulster TV. Good folks like Terry Smyth. I was also reunited with Jackie Fullerton. The camera crew were all Irish too and were top-class operators. We socialised together, along with the squad in Albuquerque.

Before we arrived in New Mexico, Doc had had a chat with the boxing promoter, Frank Warren.
Frank told him the Sheriff of Albuquerque was none other than the former light heavyweight champion of the world, Bob Foster.

Foster was boxing royalty. One of his defeats was when he stepped up a weight to fight Muhammad Ali.

So when we got there, I contacted the Sheriff's office and asked Bob if he'd do an interview.
He was most co-operative. We filmed him at a distance wearing a poncho and Stetson, badge gleaming, gun on his hip, while the Clint Eastwood theme tune played in the background. He hammed it up perfectly for his appearance on Saint and Greavsie.

At the end of our interview, he looked down the camera lens, drew his pistol and told Greavsie his kind of mischief making wouldn't be tolerated in Albuquerque. Bob looked pretty serious!

Once director Pat Pearson said "cut", Bob looked at me, a bit like Clint, and said "that goes for you too".

He was kidding. I think.

From the delights of Albuquerque, we flew to Guadalajara for the World Cup itself.

During one shoot early on, a very heavy battery charger toppled over onto the leg of our electrician Albert Kirk. It was fractured. The Doc was field producer, in charge of our team. Paul thought it was best if Albert was flown home and we got a replacement.

Albert was mortified. He was in tears at the prospect. We all pleaded with Paul to let him stay on.

"He'll be okay Chief. Once he gets a cast, we'll all muck in to carry the equipment."

Doc relented so it was "Carry On Albert".

There was a nightclub as part of the hotel complex, and one evening shortly after being patched up, Albert arrived. He wasn't on his own.

He was being given a piggy back by Norman Whiteside!

The camaraderie between the players and the TV people was second to none. It was like one big, happy family. Albert and I were stationed behind one of the goals. That gave us better access to the tunnel for post-match interviews.

At the final whistle, we set off. I wondered if we'd ever get there. Albert was on crutches, and I was carrying the lights and the battery, which wasn't exactly like a Duracell Plus. It was hot and humid. By the time we got to the end of the tunnel, I was soaked in sweat and could barely talk. Albert's leg was itching under the cast, so the first thing we had to do was find something to scratch it with.

Even so, I was delighted he was able to stay with us. Apart from being an excellent "spark", he was an integral member of the team. And always game for a laugh.

The BBC had a strong team out in Mexico. They were also based at our hotel in Guadalajara. Their producer was Brian Barwick, who became head honcho at the Beeb, ITV, the FA, rugby league and other successful operations too numerous to mention. In fact, a right clever dick. I just called him Baz.

The BBC's reporter, my opposite number, was none other than David Icke.

A former footballer himself, Icke came across as somewhat strange. Although we were staying in the same hotel, I can honestly say we never had a single conversation. We'd acknowledge each other with a nod or a quick "hi", but that was it.

One afternoon after training, he'd set up to do an interview with Pat Jennings, poolside. Curiosity got the better of me and I eavesdropped. Icke had written out every question in longhand and went through them with Pat sequentially. In other words, the answers didn't seem to matter as long as he got on to question two and so on.

A good interview is about listening to the answers, and if they're inciteful then taking it a step further, not just plough on to the next question.

At one point, Pat glanced at me with an almost apologetic look. I got the impression he didn't really want to be doing it. However, he was obliged to cooperate with the BBC as much as he was ITV. It wasn't a problem for me.

I couldn't say Icke was weird like so many people do, because I never talked to him to hear his beliefs. I just thought of him as aloof. Five years later, he claimed to be a son of Godhead, which has something to do with the Holy Trinity.

I don't mean Kendall, Ball and Harvey.

David Icke was an unusual sort of chap to say the very least.

A regular occurrence was Jackie Fullerton and I sitting at a table by the hotel bar with Big Pat and Gerry Armstrong. We'd just chew the fat and tell each other stories, but the main purpose was so Pat and Gerry could have a drink.

So there'd be four "cokes" on the table. Obviously, ours had vodka in. So too did Pat and Gerry's. But we smuggled the vodka into their cokes so if Billy Bingham walked past, he wouldn't suspect anything untoward.

It was innocent fun. It's not like they were getting pissed or anything like that. If anything, it was beneficial because it helped them sleep. It was never on the night before a match.

I have to say that the hotel was unbelievable. Each room was more like a chalet with a mini pool or hot-tub adjoining. On the drive up, you had to climb a hill. There were caged lions and tigers to deter any unwanted guests. I'd never seen anything like it.

So this particular night, the four of us were chatting away and a wedding party arrived. We nicknamed the bride horseface. Not very PC, but you work it out. Eventually Pat and Gerry left, so Jackie and I bunked in.

It turned out the bride was the daughter of the local mafia Don.

When we were being introduced to a few guests, Jackie claimed that he was a TV presenter/ commentator from Northern Ireland.

I couldn't resist.

"Stop being so modest Jackie. He's not a TV presenter at all. He's really a singer."

For the wedding entertainment, a pop group performed. Then the stage revolved and an orchestra appeared. We were looking on, when the next minute one of the "bodyguards" came down to see us.

And promptly asked Jackie to sing. He politely refused.

Five minutes later, the same bodyguard came back and TOLD him to sing. He pointed over to "Don Corleone". He made Jackie an offer he couldn't refuse.

Jackie was actually a great singer. So he got up and sang "Till", which Tom Jones recorded.

They loved him. He got a fabulous ovation. So, of course, they demanded an encore!

When Jackie had finally finished, he came back over to me for a well-deserved drink. The bodyguard had followed him. His boss loved it so much that if there was anything we wanted, we only had to ask.

Just think about it, Jackie Fullerton in the role of Johnny Fontaine, singing at The Don's daughter's wedding.

Unbelievable!

We also had a game of football against the foreign press at a very plush sports complex in Guadalajara. I burst down the right wing, and crossed for Jackie to get the winner. He was a good player. A league title winner in Northern Ireland with Crusaders.

Northern Ireland were in a difficult group alongside Algeria, Spain and Brazil. We recorded the Irish training, prior to the Spain versus Brazil opener. Afterwards we went to a technical area reserved for television personnel. I started talking to someone from TV Globo of Brazil. We hit it off and agreed to swap our footage of the Irish training for his Brazilian stuff.

We stumbled upon a secret.

Their star striker Careca had missed out in 1982, after getting injured just days before the competition started. He didn't play once in Spain. However, he was fit and ready for Mexico 86.

Careca WAS going to start this time. But Brazil wanted it kept quiet. His presence in the starting XI certainly wasn't public knowledge. The TV Globo training pictures of Careca were gold dust for us. It was our turn to provide the pictures for ITV back home. Everything had to go via Mexico City before reaching London.

The rain began to fall. It got louder and louder on the roof of where we were. Then within seconds, a massive storm arrived. And it killed our link to Mexico City. We wouldn't be able to send our stuff to London.

In Doc's eyes, there was only one person to blame.

God!

Paul was livid. We had these great clips of Brazil and Careca. And we couldn't use it.

Or could we?

Our engineer was Jim Andrew, from Yorkshire TV. The Doc knew him and Jim had been with us in 1982 as well. Jim piped up:

"Remember when we were going to that sports complex for the football match the other day? It was in the rich part of Guadalajara. Can you get us up there?"

All the houses we'd seen had big gardens. In each one was a giant, and I mean huge, satellite dish. It might've been the early days of satellite, but these folks all had one. We climbed on our bus and told the driver where we wanted to go. As we arrived in this residential area, Jim pointed randomly at a house.

I had no idea what he was trying to do. But Jim clearly had a plan. The Doc went to the house. Luckily when the door was answered, the person had a little bit of English. And he was happy to help. Jim wanted to use his satellite dish.

The storm was a lot calmer now, it had gone back to heavy rain. Jim got his toolbox out. He took a plate off the dish, so he could get to the inner workings of it. Jim then connected the camera to the dish via a cable. At the same time, The Doc was on the phone to Mexico City to tell them what was going on. They confirmed that they had a still image from us. A button was pressed and the video began.

It was working!

We didn't use the Northern Ireland clips, only the Careca stuff. The most important part was to preview Brazil versus Spain. Paul was ecstatic. And Jim Andrew was the hero of the hour. The Doc loved it when someone displayed ingenuity or improvisation, who went above and beyond. He loved that as much as, if not more than, anything else.

The Doc wanted to celebrate. He announced that he was going to take us out. We were drenched of course, but with the hotel not so far away, we were able to get changed first. We went to one of the biggest hotels in the city. It was jam packed with Brazilian fans. And the majority were women. Beautiful women.

We managed to get through the sea of people. The drinks were on The Doc. Well ITV anyway! I glanced around the bar, noticing that it'd already gone past midnight. It was now the day of the Brazil versus Spain game.

That's when I saw two familiar faces. They were dancing away and having a great time.

Socrates and Junior!!

I couldn't believe it. I was trying to get Paul's attention. He was too deep into a conversation about cables, dishes and feeds. The Doc finally saw what I was seeing. His first reaction?

"Have we got a camera? Where's the camera?"

We didn't have anything.

Seeing the Brazil captain and one of their other star players bopping on the dance floor made me want to put a Peso or two on Spain.

It's a good job I didn't. It finished Brazil 1 Spain 0.

Who scored the winner?

Socrates!

We didn't stay out in Mexico too long. Northern Ireland took only one point from their three matches and were eliminated.

Before we left, there was time to wish Pat Jennings a happy 41st birthday and celebrate his retirement from football. Jackie and Terry organised a small party for Pat. We tried our best to get Pelé to present the cake to him. He was in Mexico City though, so it was just too difficult for Pelé to come to Guadalajara.

We did manage to find one Brazilian legend though; Clodoaldo. The man who started the move for that famous Carlos Alberto goal in the 1970 World Cup final. When we asked him to make the presentation, he was delighted. It was lovely surprise for Big Pat when Clodoaldo walked in and gave him the cake.

We might not have got Pelé but it didn't matter. We all had a superb time. Especially Pat.

20

A good sport

When you're an actor, you don't want to be typecast. Some people might say the same thing about TV presenters. I was more than happy to just do football, I love the game. But unlike others who've only ever covered one sport, I did more than that. The bowls came from nowhere and became cult viewing. There were other gigs too.

I got involved with snooker and it turned out to be perfect timing. I presented The Lada Classic in Oldham in 1982. It was exclusively on Granada. It was there that Steve Davis performed the first televised 147 break in his match against John Spencer. As we had the footage of the first ever televised maximum, The Doc had an idea.

Paul called Barry Hearn and told him what had happened. The Doc wanted to turn it into a video. With the new explosion of VHS cassettes on the market, both of them saw it as a money spinner. They agreed on the terms of the deal and out it went. As the 147 had only been shown in the North West, the tape was a big success. A lot of people had never seen it before.

Firstly, the break was shown in its entirety with the original commentary. Co-commentator David Taylor got a bit carried away and was urging Steve on at the end. David knew that history was being made.

After that, the break was repeated. But this time it was with Steve and I talking through every shot. He could recall each one. The he'd explain what he was thinking to prepare for the next one. It was fascinating stuff.

Steve still jokes about that famous moment.

"When someone gets a 147 today, they win a fortune. All I got was a Lada car!"

I enjoyed doing the video with Steve. He was often labelled "boring". I can tell you that he certainly wasn't.

One snooker player who was never boring; Alex "Hurricane" Higgins.

Like George Best, Alex was another genius from Belfast. There were other similarities between them outside of sport too. Higgins was never far from the news, and his behaviour was certainly erratic at times. He was a superb snooker player but he just couldn't resist a drink.

I first met Alex at Old Trafford at a Manchester United game. He was a big United supporter. He came over to me and introduced himself. We hit it off immediately.

Then, out of the blue, he asked me to call him "Sandy". He explained that his family back home in Northern Ireland called him that.

Later on, he was playing an exhibition match in Manchester. There was an afternoon session and then later, an evening one. His opponent was John Spencer, a former world champion. I'd been asked to do the introductions. There was an interval of about two hours before the evening session. Alex lived locally so he asked me to go back to his place for a bit. His wife Lynn made us a meal. Needless to say, Alex had a drink.

Then from nowhere he said "watch this". He got up and put on a video tape of his favourite clips from Kungfu movies. We sat there and watched it for about 45 minutes. Alex was doing the actions and the noises. He knew it off by heart.

"Look at this!"

"POW!"

"Watch what he does here!"

"HEE-YAH!"

Then we went back for the evening session. He finished the match, and beat John Spencer. In front of a full house. Alex was the people's champion. They loved him.

Not long after that, he was doing another exhibition game. This one was against Steve Davis at the Saint George's Hall in Liverpool. So Alex rang me up, knowing I didn't live that far away. He invited me to come and watch. I wasn't working. I just went to see him play Steve.

The interval arrived and Alex came over:

"Let's go for a drink. Where we gonna go for a drink?"

"Well, the nearest is 'The Legs of Man'. It's virtually opposite here."

I knew the place. I'd been in before. It was run by a lady, just known as "Sadie". So we went in. We found the best side and Sadie saw us come in.

"I'm really sorry Elton but you can't go in the posh side without a tie on."

I was dressed casually in a t-shirt and Alex wasn't wearing a tie either. But she had a rack of ties hanging behind the bar. So she pulled two ties off the rack and told us to put them on. We didn't have to tie them, just put them around us. It looked ridiculous. But nobody could say we weren't following the rules.

Alex started on the vodka and, as I wasn't working, I joined in. Then this woman came in from the tap room. She'd seen us through the gap between the two rooms. She started to stare at Alex, who was just sitting there, having a drink with me. She came over. She was a little giddy to say the least.

"Ah, Mr Higgins! Oh God! Just to meet you! Oh fantastic! Oh great! I only watch snooker if you're playing. You know what I mean? Yer great. Just, I just. Just to be in your company is magnificent. Can I've your autograph?"

"Fuck off!"

Oh God! I knew what we had to do next. Leg it!

"We're out of here."

I had to drag him out of the place and back to Saint George's Hall. I don't know who she was with, but Alex could have got his head kicked in. And so could I. Guilty by association.

During the 1980s, darts became extremely popular. It was still considered a pub game by some, but the players were now household names. The likes of Eric Bristow, John Lowe and Jocky Wilson. And they'd enjoy a pint and a smoke DURING their matches. The game show Bullseye certainly helped as well. I worked on the darts and it was certainly something else. Nothing like it is today, with thousands of fans, giant screens and razzamatazz.

One night, I was at The Queen Elizabeth Hall in Oldham for a tournament. The same venue where Steve Davis got that 147. I was going live into Midweek Sports Special. The show was networked from Thames TV, linking into matches played earlier in the evening. All the darts had been recorded and had already finished.

As I was doing my links, things took a turn for the worse downstairs.

I don't know who or what caused it but there was a riot going on. Tables and chairs were being thrown all over the place. There were glasses of beer in mid-air. Guys were bleeding. It was like something from the Wild West.

I had to carry on as if nothing was happening.

The folks in the gallery at Thames didn't know what was going on either. They could hear the noise as I was talking to the nation. Eventually, the police arrived while I was still live on air. It was total chaos.

As always, the show had to go on.

Away from bar room brawls, I dipped my toe into boxing too. And I was in the right place at the right time when a British boxer made history. Jim Rosenthal was ill, so I presented the fight from the LWT studios between Lloyd Honeygan and Don Curry.

Taking place in Atlantic City, and for the undisputed welterweight championship, Honeygan was a massive underdog. So much so, that some bookies refused to take bets on the fight. Nobody expected Curry to lose.

I wasn't that schooled in the sport to be honest. The producer Stewart McConachie must've wondered who he'd been lumbered with when I asked him "what's the tale of the tape?" Anyway, as it turned out, the programme was a massive success. Against all the odds, Honeygan won. It was one of the biggest shocks in boxing history at the time.

Reg Gutteridge was the voice of boxing for ITV and I was delighted to be part of the same broadcast as he was such a legend. He was a larger-than-life character who lost a leg during the war. But not everyone knew that. Reg became close to Muhammad Ali and would tell stories about "the greatest".

Once Reg was enjoying Ali's company at a dinner. And Ali was in full flow.

"I'm the greatest. I'm so pretty. There's no-one tougher than me."

At which point, Reg grabbed a knife and turned to Ali.

"Are you as tough as this?"

Reg then stabbed himself. In his wooden leg.

Ali didn't know about the wooden leg! Reg only had a slight limp so you'd never guess. It was quickly explained to Ali, who was relieved to know he was still the toughest of all time!

Okay, so I was no boxing aficionado but I still enjoyed it. My good pal and colleague Gary Newbon was the oracle of the sweet science. Gary was a big advocate for boxing on ITV. He was good friends with The Doc too.

Gary was very versatile and did a lot of sport on TV. He even once stepped in for me at the bowls. He did an excellent job. But football and boxing were his two biggest passions. He liked a laugh, but when he was doing his job he was a serious professional. Maybe too serious. So when it was his birthday one year, we decided to rib him.

We were doing an amateur boxing event on Merseyside. The Doc liked to work with Gary when he could, so he had him doing the interviews. As it was Gary's birthday, we told him that someone from a local religious organisation was going to make a presentation in the ring.

Or so he thought.

A nun stepped up with a big cardboard cheque, made out to a local children's home. Gary was already stood on the canvas waiting for her. As she climbed up the steps, her habit slightly split open, revealing fishnet tights. She was also wearing bright red lipstick and eyeshadow.

Do you see where this is going?

Gary Newbon didn't.

She gave him the cheque, which he accepted on behalf of the charity. As he was looking down at it, the nun took off her headwear. She shook her hair. He looked up and finally realised. This was no ordinary nun. It wasn't Whoopie Goldberg either!

It'd been so obvious to everyone that she was a strippergram.

Except to Gary!

21

Euro 88

The domestic football season came to a close in May 1988. We covered the FA Cup final when Wimbledon shocked league champions Liverpool 1-0 to win it. I even had the chance to speak to Cloughie on air. He was in the bar at Wembley; dead chuffed.

Young Nigel had just been presented with the Barclays Young Eagle Award. Brian spoke like a proud dad. Not as his manager at Nottingham Forest.

"It'll be the first and last time he gets the headlines instead of ME."

He couldn't resist throwing in a bit of typical Cloughie.

A few weeks before the Wimbledon victory, we covered Luton Town's dramatic 3-2 win over Arsenal in the Littlewood's Cup Final. That's what the League Cup was called at the time. Brian Moore's words are part of that famous day in Luton's history. Mooro rose to the occasion for both finals. It was arguably my favourite Wembley final as a neutral.

Although I was friendly with Brian, we didn't socialise together very often. There weren't any issues; Brian was very private and older than me, that's all. The running joke at ITV though was how careful Mooro was with money.

That summer in West Germany for Euro 88, I went shopping with him. He was desperate for some comfy new shoes. When he finally found some, he was delighted. He never took them off! Jimmy Greaves used to always joke about Mooro being a bit tight.

After being at the previous two World Cups, Euro 88 was to be my first European championship. ITV didn't even cover Euro 84. None of the British nations or Ireland were there. So they didn't bother.

For Euro 88, my role was reporter for the Irish squad, managed by proud Englishman and World Cup winner Jack Charlton. Big Jack was already a hero in Ireland just for achieving qualification. Thousands of fans would now make their way over for the tournament. Their first ever. The Irish supporters were going to have a good craic.

So were the players!

As part of the buildup, I went to Dublin to meet Jack and his assistant Maurice Setters. As I've already mentioned, I first met Jack back in 1977 but there was no way he remembered that. He wasn't good with names.

From the moment we walked into the first pub, Big Jack was mobbed. I'd never seen anything like it. The locals treated him like a god. Everyone wanted to buy him a drink. We couldn't pay for a round if we tried. It was incredible.

Jack embraced the Irish culture. Well, the Guinness anyway. He insisted I sample a REAL pint of it. I was in a bit of a quandary though. I didn't like Guinness; I had a half to be polite. From that first night out in Dublin, the foundations of our friendship were laid. Jack and I had chemistry.

I was intrigued why Jack took the Ireland job. Back in 1977, after leaving Middlesbrough, Big Jack wanted to replace Don Revie as England manager. He'd done well at Ayresome Park but felt he'd taken the club as far as he could. The timing seemed perfect for Jack. So he applied for the job.

"I went for it. The bastards never even sent me a letter back."

What a way to treat a national hero. This was Jack Charlton, World Cup winner. It was disgraceful. At the same time the FA also turned down Brian Clough. Ron Greenwood was chosen instead. The FA got it wrong.

Jack didn't say as much, but the whole situation hurt him.

"I never applied for any job after that."

He didn't need to. He was always in demand. How different things could've been if Jack or Cloughie had been appointed at the end of the 1970s.

With only eight teams competing at Euro 88, it wasn't a big shock to see Ireland in the same group as England. It was also the opening game for each country. And live on ITV. The story wrote itself. Ireland, the underdogs, led by an Englishman. Club mates against each other. There were Irish lads who were born in England too. Jack had done a great job rounding up players who qualified through a relation.

Or they owned an Irish Wolfhound.

After bonding in Dublin, I was confident my new friendship with Jack would help me a lot at Euro 88. Remember when I was with Northern Ireland in Spain and Mexico? Billy Bingham let me film on the team coach. When I got to West Germany, I asked Big Jack if I could do the same.

"No fuckin' way!"

As this was the 1980s, there was a lot of fear of football hooliganism overshadowing the competition. The British government were particularly vocal about the problem and pointed the finger firmly at the English fans. Outside the stadium in Stuttgart for the England versus Ireland match, I cornered Sports Minister Colin Moynihan. He'd been at the forefront of bringing in identity cards for supporters. At 5 ft 2", he was known as the "Miniature for Sport".

I got straight to the point.

"What are you going to do about the hooliganism problem?"

He replied that if there was any trouble, then he'd make the England team go home immediately. It was powerful stuff. The press followed up the story the next day.

Thankfully it didn't happen.

In the studio in London, Nick Owen was presenting with Ian St. John and Cloughie as guests. Saint was friends with Big Jack and Maurice Setters. Ian had worked with both of them at Sheffield Wednesday. He believed the Irish had a real chance. As a Scotsman, he wanted them to win.

Cloughie was Cloughie – pinpointing Mick McCarthy as the weakest link.

"Lineker and Beardsley will be rubbing their hands."

The comments backfired. Mick McCarthy was one of Ireland's heroes as they beat England 1-0 through Ray Houghton's goal.

And they held a huge party to celebrate. It was wild!

At first it was strange being there because England had lost. We didn't record any of the celebrations. That was never going to happen. I interviewed Jack and that was it. After that, we both joined in with the squad. I knew a lot of them already. Players like Ronnie Whelan, John Aldridge, Paul McGrath. It was some night!

The Irish did really well in the tournament. They drew 1-1 with the Soviet Union in their second game. Ronnie Whelan scored a wonderful goal in that one. Just a draw against Holland would see them advance. They were minutes from the semi-final until the Dutch scored late on. That 1-0 defeat eliminated Ireland. England were out too after losing all three matches.

There were two semi-finals and the final left to play. Despite originally being just there to cover the Irish, I was to stay until the very end of the competition. Holland knocked out hosts West Germany, setting up a final against the Soviet Union, who beat Italy. The final was to be a repeat of their opening group game. The Soviets had won that 1-0.

Thanks to Martin Tyler, I was able to interview an all-time great. Rinus Michels had revitalised the Dutch. The concept of Total Football was his brainchild in the 1960s and 1970s. He couldn't have been so successful without Johan Cruyff, who was the orchestrator on the pitch. At this time, Michels wasn't speaking to the Dutch media so the likelihood of him sitting down in conversation with me was pretty slim.

Martin was friendly with a commentator for Dutch TV, who was well in with Michels. It was arranged for Michels to be smuggled into a hotel room so we could meet and do an interview. It was real cloak and dagger stuff.

Michels turned out to be a joy.

When I asked a straight question, I got a straight answer. Prior to the semi-final, Michels hadn't been entirely happy. I asked him if he had any reservations about his team. He said yes and it was due to their fighting qualities.

Or lack of.

"What worries me, if needs be, there's only one of my players who'd risk getting a yellow card for the good of the team."

I asked him which one.

"Jan Wouters."

He said it just like that. No hesitation. I'm pretty sure I've never interviewed a manager or coach who would voluntarily divulge such information. He went up even further in my estimation, which puts him pretty high on my list of great managers to interview.

Incidentally, Wouters was the guy who elbowed Gazza at Wembley in 1993. As a result, Paul had to play a number of games in a Phantom of the Opera style mask.

Before the final, our group of six – the camera crew, producer Robert Charles, interpreter Susie and myself –

went to Munich. We had a couple of days to kill. On the first afternoon, Bob Charles disappeared. When he returned, he said:

"Get yourselves ready. We're going out."

We all piled into a minibus and drove into Munich to a Bier Keller.

This was no ordinary Bier Keller.

It was a Dinkelacker Bier Keller.

What's Dinkelacker? The German lager, brewed in Stuttgart, where we'd been based on our arrival in West Germany. It was delicious. We had a great night. We all got on so well. It was a shame our trip was nearly over.

I remember it vividly. There was a suckling pig on the table. And jugs of Dinkelacker!

Next up the final.

I'd been to the pre-match press conference, and literally queued to interview Ruud Gullit. He was so affable. In for a penny, I asked him if he'd do an interview, on the pitch, if the Dutch were doing a victory lap of honour.

"Sure."

"I'll be squatting behind the goal. I'll wave."

Sounds ridiculous, but if you don't ask you don't get!

The game itself was largely dominated by the Dutch. Gullit, who had a real aura about him, scored the first. He was running the game. And then came a moment I'll never forget. I was behind the goal that the Dutch were attacking in the second half.

The strike that defined Euro 88. And I got a worm's-eye view.

Arnold Murhen sent in a deep cross towards Marco van Basten. His focus was incredible. As the ball dropped, Van Basten connected from a tight angle. And it flew in.

I had such an excellent viewpoint, I swear I ducked!

I couldn't believe it. A jaw-dropping moment if ever there was one. The Dutch were champions of Europe. And embarked on a lap of honour in front of thousands of fans. All clad in bright orange. Gullit was holding the cup. I moved in.

Then in my ear I heard:

"No Elt, Don't do it. Let it go!"

I was probably about 20 yards away from Gullit, but had to back off. It was extremely disappointing at the time. But I understood when it was explained to me later. ITV didn't want to aggravate UEFA ahead of negotiations for the TV rights for the European club competitions.

It was the right decision.

With the final over, we had one last hurrah in a different Bier Keller. The ITV team turned out in force. For a night of grub, wine and beer. Our group were regarded as the party ring leaders. We'd been practising for the best part of four weeks.

Work hard, play hard was our motto.

One stunt that had confounded the locals – whether in Stuttgart, Hamburg or Munich – involved a bottle of Cointreau. The trick is to soak your index finger in saliva, dip it into a glass of Cointreau and set fire to it. Then stick it in your mouth to extinguish the flame. It really doesn't hurt at all.

However:

DO NOT TRY THIS AT HOME

Our interpreter Susie demonstrated how to do it. I introduced her as Susie Cointreau! Think about it.

Everyone had a go and thought it was a good laugh. I say everyone. One abstained. Mooro was one of the first to try it, but the one who wouldn't was Big Ron Atkinson. He was too busy sipping champagne.

All in all, it was a fabulous trip. I thoroughly enjoyed West Germany and its culture.

Life was good.

22

I know you got Seoul

I'll be honest with you, I cringe if people say that I'm or was a "celebrity". I worked my way up, took the opportunities that came my way and managed to get on both the radio and the telly. Great.

In the 1980s, when I was presenting live football, I just saw myself as a bloke doing a job he loved. Nothing more. In 1988, I was offered another presenting role by ITV. I was chosen to be the lead anchor for the overnight coverage of 1988 Seoul Olympics in South Korea.

With the time difference, it was going to be gruelling work. But I relished the challenge and I knew I was going to be the person breaking the big stories.

There were plenty of them.

It's funny because a lot of people don't know or remember me doing the games that year. I wonder why! How many of you stayed up through the night to watch it? There are always certain events that people want to see such as the Men's 100 m final but I'm not sure it's the same for some of the more obscure ones. Especially when they're on at between 2 am and 6 am.

So why me?

I later heard that executive producer Adrian Metcalfe suggested me for the job because it would require a lot of "sports hopping". That meant switching from one event to other as things developed. I do believe my reputation for ad-libbing didn't do me any harm either. I was also told that I was considered a bit of a "Jack the lad" with a cheeky Scouse humour. That humour came out a fair bit during the games.

Before the games began though, ITV wanted to drum up some interest. They wanted to promote their coverage to a mainstream audience. The idea was to put a group of the presenters on The Krypton Factor against a team of ex-Olympians.

The Krypton Factor was a game show that pitted contestants against each other in physical and mental challenges. It was very popular and it was helped by having an excellent host. Gordon Burns was someone I knew well from Granada and he even did some Kick Off stuff. I liked Gordon and he was so good at everything he did. The Krypton Factor was a huge success and ran for years.

So who was on my team? Firstly, ITV Sport legend Dickie Davies. Dickie was 60 at the time so he wasn't going to be taking part in the obstacle course bit. But he was as sharp as a tack and would prove handy in the other rounds. Then there was Nick Owen. He was another master of his trade, who was equally at home doing breakfast TV, the news or different sports.

Finally, there was Alison Holloway. Alison had been working in television since she was a teenager but had become more famous because of her marriage to comedian Jim Davidson. She was in the tabloids a lot during this time as her relationship with Davidson was falling apart.

It was a brilliant experience and I'm particularly pleased with how I did on the obstacle course. I won my heat. Our team triumphed overall and it gave us some publicity before the games began. We only had four channels back then and millions watched The Krypton Factor.

Now it was time for the Olympic Games.

You're probably thinking that I was fortunate to be in South Korea. Wrong. I was in a studio in London. The only colleagues in Seoul where the commentators, reporters and production staff. Myself and the team of experts worked through the night from Thames TV. That's why it was so hard.

I know a lot of people work nights on a regular basis. Ask them about it. It's gruelling. I did it back when I was at Broadgreen Hospital in Liverpool. I was lucky because me and the other porters used to cover for each other. We'd get some mattresses and take it in turns to sleep. During the night, there wasn't much to do. Being live on television was a lot different. There was no hiding place.

The team I worked with made it easier though. We became a real unit together. There were some well-known names.

Barry Norman would begin proceedings before passing over to me. Barry would do an hour or so and then I'd do the rest. Barry had an excellent reputation for his TV work, and his film show on BBC was a big hit for many years. Good guy.

I don't mean to be cruel though when I say that being a live sports presenter wasn't his strongest point. The safety blanket of pre-recorded television wasn't there for him. He ended up doing less than originally planned. It became clear that he wasn't so comfortable when the news started coming in thick and fast from Seoul. There was a lot going on at the same time and Barry wasn't used to it. Put him in front of Robert De Niro or Al Pacino, talking about their latest project. No problem for Barry.

One night, he was told to go to a break. He didn't know what to do. He was lost. I wasn't on camera but one of the producers, Phil King, was screaming at me to help Barry out.

I walked on to the set.

"Barry, we're going to a break now. This is how we do it in Liverpool."

I put on a Scouse accent.

"'Ere are the adverts."

We had another Barry on the sofa. Boxer Barry McGuigan. Suzanne Dando had been a champion gymnast but after retiring young, she became a celebrity. She had a lot of male fans!

Then there was Harvey Smith, our equestrian expert. With Harvey by my side, we became something of a double-act. Harvey, a no-nonsense Yorkshireman, always said what he thought.

For example, after the dressage had finished.

"What did you think of that Harvey?"

"Notta lot."

"Is that it?"

"Yeah. Yeah. Hosses. Hosses are meant to run or jump. They're not BLOODY ballet dancers."

Everyone else on the couch agreed. That left me with 45 seconds to fill, telling everyone at home what was coming up next. I went to break and everyone laughed out loud. It was a bloody wind up!

Harvey had made the papers back in the 1971, when he gave the V-sign to the judges after winning British Show Jumping Derby. Of course he denied it.

"It was a straightforward V for victory. Churchill used it throughout the war."

The judges were having none of it. Harvey was stripped of the title and fined £2,000. That was a lot of money back then. He was a rebel and he made the sport more popular. As I got to know him better, I introduced him one night as "The Alex Higgins of showjumping".

Long before she did "A Question of Sport", Sue Barker joined us on the panel. What a natural. Sue was there to talk about Steffi Graf mainly. She had her leg pulled a few times but she didn't mind one bit.

We were going to a commercial break when the bacon butties arrived. The highlight of Harvey's night! He was a food critic. Specialist subject? Bacon butties. We tucked in during the break, eating as fast as we could before being back on air. Sue still hadn't finished when we resumed the show.

I couldn't resist it.

"Sue, a final word on Steffi Graf?"

She nearly choked on the bacon butty!

I got Sue again when the three-day eventing came to a conclusion.

"Mark Todd there, winning gold with Charisma. Sue told me that the horse has more of it than the rider."

"Elton! Don't say that!"

"Too late, I've already said it."

Sue was in stitches. It was 5 am, we got away with it.

Athletics was represented well. We had Steve Ovett, Roger Black and Alan Wells. Black was injured and couldn't compete in Seoul but he didn't let it get him down. He was lots of fun.

One night we were doing synchronised swimming. It was a trial event for the Olympics. It was also boring. I had to interview the doyenne of synchronised swimming in our country, Heather Etherington. While she was speaking, Blackie whispered something in my ear that I cannot repeat in this book.

It was a filthy joke. Filthy but very funny! While Heather continued, Blackie and I had a fit of the giggles. Poor Heather didn't know what was going on.

There was rowing expert Dan Topolski. He was probably the lesser known of the panel but Great Britain were excellent at this sport and won many a gold medal. Dan was lucky if he saw much of the games though, he used to nod off. He wasn't on camera that much and found it hard to adjust to working through the night. If there was no rowing on, we left Dan to sleep. When it was time for him to speak, I had to ask whoever was next to Dan to wake him up.

Dan was having a nap while we were on air, when Steve Ovett intervened. Steve blew into a crisp packet, filling it with air. Then he put it next to Dan's ear. Steve burst it, making an almighty bang. Poor Dan jumped out of his skin in shock.

I won't deny that at times I was very tired. It's like marathon running, where you hit the wall. You have to find that bit extra. Four nights in, on 20th September, it was my daughter Laura's 4th birthday. At the end of my shift, she'd be awake and so I knew that I could wish her happy birthday on air.

We were scheduled to finish at 8 am, and then hand over to the next team, led by Nick Owen. Before Nick began, it was many happy returns time to Laura.

"Hpbrthdy Lra."

No, that wasn't it.

"Laubrthdyhppy."

That wasn't right either. I tried again.

"Halrabhthy."

I couldn't get my words out. I was really tired. I had nothing left. The more I tried to wish her happy birthday, the more the words jumbled into one. It was horrible. My brain was so fried.

Cue Nick.

Nick leaned on me and said:

"Happy Birthday Laura from all of us. Have a wonderful day."

Nick delivered it perfectly. He hadn't been up all night though, had he?

We could certainly get away with a lot more than normal because we were working through the night. There were a lot of inside jokes, cheeky comments and innuendos. At times it was like a Carry On film. Nobody ever told us what the ratings were.

Or for that matter, how to behave.

Sometimes we had to report on serious matters. The biggest story of the games revolved around the Men's 100 m final. Carl Lewis had dominated the 1984 Olympics in Los Angeles and many expected him to win another gold at this event in South Korea. Britain's representative was Linford Christie, while Canadian Ben Johnson and Lewis were fierce rivals. Former world record holder Calvin Smith was also tipped for a medal. The bar had never been higher.

The final was a classic. Johnson beat Lewis to the gold, setting a new world record of 9.79 seconds. We'd seen history made right before our eyes. Christie came in third and took the bronze. We were all delighted for Linford, while recognising how unlucky he was to be a sprinter in an era of true greats like Johnson and Lewis.

We didn't think about the final again afterwards, there were plenty of other events to keep us occupied. But while on air a couple of days later, I had to deal with some breaking news that shook the Olympics to its very foundations.

Before I knew what was going on, I was confused by a vision coming from the corner of my eye. John McCririck, the well-known horse racing pundit, was working with us behind the scenes. As I was speaking into the camera, I saw John slithering across the floor.

Beached whale came to mind. He managed to stay out of sight while handing me a piece of paper. I had no idea what was on the sheet. John had set off again on his belly, which was a sight and a half. I had to hold it together.

I read out the news that Ben Johnson had failed a drug test and had been stripped of his gold medal. It was unprecedented for the 100 m final, arguably the most prestigious event of the games. That meant Lewis took gold, Linford got upgraded to silver and Smith was awarded the bronze.

Phil King had the idea to link up with Canada to see their reaction. It seemed crazy at the time. But getting their perspective and putting it on air would set us apart. We established a link with Canadian TV. We had no contact with them directly. We didn't know what time the titles would begin for their news show. We knew they were coming up, that's all.

Would it be in ten seconds or ten minutes? That was my problem. Then just like that, the Canadian news began and I shut up. The Ben Johnson failed drug test was enormous in 1988. It was front and back-page news.

Not long after, Linford Christie was then rocked after failing a test of his own when competing in the 200 m. Christie declared his innocence. Believing Linford, Jim Rosenthal played Lieutenant Columbo and investigated how Christie had tested positive for a banned substance. Jim led the campaign to clear Linford's name. In the end, it was traced to ginseng tea that Linford had drunk. He was given the benefit of the doubt and he was able to compete.

With us being in London and the action live in South Korea, there were always going to be moments where things didn't go as planned. Remember how I was good at "sports hopping"? Well, we "hopped" at a really inappropriate time. The British men's hockey team were playing their semi-final.

With the game at a vital moment, we cut off to another event. We missed the conclusion. I wasn't happy, neither was my pal Jim Ramsey, who was producing in Seoul. He was hopping mad. Jippo, as he was known, didn't pull any punches. I had to do what I was told and get on with it. Britain won that game, and then got gold after beating West Germany in the final.

As we came to the last show of the games, I was told that I deserved a break and so I wouldn't be needed for the live broadcast.

"Let your hair down Elton."

My sofa mates, who'd been with me through the nights, insisted that I go live with them. As I'd had a few drinks, I'd lost any inhibitions. So I went and did the programme. I sat there, trying to be on my best behaviour. I failed.

Dickie Davies did a speech that went something along these lines:

"We've really had a great Olympics. We've certainly enjoyed it here on ITV. Elton here, was through the night. Did you enjoy it Elton?"

"Yeah, yeah I did. Have you heard about the nudist Olympics? In the 4x100 m relay, a fella got dragged 20 yards!"

There was a pause before people started laughing. I wasn't done though.

"Did you hear about the Irish Olympics? Catching the javelin and heading the shot!"

I didn't care. The studio was in uproar. My material would probably be deemed inappropriate today. It was out of the Frank Carson school of comedy.

There was a fair bit of drinking during our Olympics coverage but this was first time any of us had been live while under the influence. After we finished the night shift, it was common for us to unwind and have a few drinks. I was doing just that when ITV's main man Greg Dyke came into the green room. Greg was a supporter of mine. Then he saw me having a drink at 10 am.

He asked Bob Burrows, who was head of sport for Thames Television, for a word.

"I'm not too happy about this, everybody drinking at ten o'clock in the morning."

Bob, who was head of sport, defended us all.

"They've been working all night. This is like ten at night for them."

That's the way we saw it too, Bob.

After we finished our drinks, a few of us walked back to the hotel. We were nearly there when a car came speeding around the corner, almost on two wheels. We were nearly knocked flying. The car went into the hotel car park. We caught it up and because I'd had a few drinks, I opened up.

"You twat! You nearly fucking killed us! Fuck off!"

The door opened.

The "twat" was Frank Bruno.

"Morning Frank, alright?"

Frank was a guest on the morning show with Nick and Alison. Six months later, Frank had lesser opposition than me.

Mike Tyson!

Doing the Olympics proved to be such a great experience. We had a lot of fun and got away with murder.

What a year 1988 had been so far.

And it wasn't done yet.

23

Never a dull Sunday

1988 continued to be a huge year for ITV when they negotiated with the Football League for the exclusive rights to show English top flight games. This meant not only live matches but cameras at every ground. It meant that we would be able to show every goal.

Over on the BBC, they could only broadcast FA Cup matches. Match of the Day was now going to be a rarity. It would only consist of cup ties. They had highlights of Kettering Town versus Bristol Rovers. ITV had live coverage of Manchester United versus Liverpool. There was a lot of positivity around the channel.

I was still doing the results service. I'd also done some live First Division games on Sunday afternoons. Don't forget the cup finals either. That was before the deal was agreed though. Who would be the face of the new coverage? The Doc was campaigning for me.

I wasn't confident. As I've already said, it was a political minefield. The suits had their favourites. It was a brilliant opportunity for someone. One person who was keen on the job was Ian St. John. He didn't get it.

John "Brommers" Bromley broke the news. I was going to be the presenter of The Match. I was thrilled and a trifle shocked. Brommers then sent for Jeff Foulser, who was going to be the executive producer. We didn't get off to the best of starts.

"Well, I wanted Jim Rosenthal, but we'll just have to get on with it."

It was an insensitive thing to say. It didn't give me a lot of confidence about our working relationship. But I had the job. The general feeling was that it was better to have an experienced presenter rather than an ex-footballer. That took The Saint out of the equation.

Ian wasn't too happy about the decision. That became clear when I had dinner with Saint, Granada's Richard Signy and Bob Patience, who was the producer of Saint and Greavsie.

We were at a Chinese restaurant on the South Bank and the topic got around to potential England goalkeepers. I was surprised that Martin Hodge of Sheffield Wednesday, formerly of Everton, was never mentioned in the press in connection with the number one position. That's all I said.

The Saint let me have it. I'd never seen him like this before. He went on a rant about me choosing Hodge because I was a bluenose. It was ridiculous and he was getting out of hand. He'd really lost the plot.

He threatened to chin me.

All over my thoughts about Martin Hodge? There was more to it than that. There had to be.

If Ian was annoyed about me doing the job he wanted, I wasn't the person to blame. I accepted a role that was offered to me. But he was ready to stick one on me. Thankfully Richard and Bob were there to make sure it didn't happen. We stayed cordial but things were never the same after that.

When the first live fixture was announced, the preparation began. Some things were different, some stayed the same. The opening titles and music changed. They had to. We needed a new, fresh look. We couldn't be the same as in previous seasons when we shared the TV rights with the BBC. In the past, the live games had also been called "The Big Match Live".

What inventive and exciting title would this exclusive new content have now?

"The Match."

That must have taken hours to come up with.

There was one constant. Brian Moore was still on commentary. He was the number one on ITV and with good reason. Occasionally Alan Parry and Martin Tyler would deputise for Brian.

The first game was on Sunday 30th October. The season was already well underway by this point. It was from Goodison Park, which made me happy. But Everton were struggling down in 15th and opponents Manchester United were 12th. Everton had been champions as recently as 1987. The previous season, United had also finished second to Liverpool.

All the hallmarks of a classic.

It wasn't.

Two big-money summer signings were on the scoresheet though. Mark Hughes scored acrobatically for United before Tony Cottee levelled shortly after. Our new technology, which involved a camera in the back of the net, was able to catch both goals from different angles. It was a first.

We were off and running.

Although we'd embraced new ideas, we didn't spend a lot of time before kick-off analysing the teams. All the First Division goals from the previous day were shown at half-time or full-time, which I provided the majority of the voiceovers for.

This was an era where people spoke a lot more candidly.

Naturally, one of the best guests for that was Brian Clough.

By now I knew Brian fairly well and we had a good relationship. When he first really warmed to me was during Midweek Sports Special. He was Brian Moore's guest. I was sat in another part of the studio, with the news of the day. I got to the last item, which was about Cloughie's son Nigel.

"Nigel Clough will miss Nottingham Forest's next game because he has chicken pox. And that's one reason why I'm sitting over here and Brian is over there."

Cloughie burst into laughter. If I had to pinpoint one moment where we connected, that was it.

Brian Clough had already appeared on Kick Off before this, when he came face to face with Polish goalkeeper Jan Tomaszewski.

Back in 1973, Cloughie had labelled Tomaszewski a clown during and after a vital World Cup qualifier between England and Poland. It was disrespectful and the comment stayed with the keeper throughout his career. Of course, Tomaszewski had a blinder at Wembley, and England could only draw 1-1. That wasn't enough, so there was no World Cup for England in 1974.

Years later on Kick Off, we had a segment called "Save of the Season". We debated on who should judge it. Then The Doc had an idea.

"How about Brian Clough and Jan Tomaszewski?"

We thought Doc's idea was great but impossible.

Wrong.

We got in touch with Tomaszewski through Kazimierz Deyna, who'd played for Manchester City. Through an interpreter, he got him to not only come for the show, but to learn broken English in a matter of six weeks. Cloughie was right up for it. So we did it. Clough, Tomaszewski and me in the studio together.

Of course, we played the clip of Cloughie tearing into the keeper and calling him a clown. Then I asked Brian what he thought of that now.

"I was out of order. In fact, that was cruel. You were great for your country on the night and I apologise young man."

So I turned to Tomaszewski and asked him for his thoughts. He replied:

"Zen Bree-an speak, zen think. Now Bree-an think, zen speak."

Cloughie had to reply.

"What his name? Gan?"

Cloughie had taken the hump because a man who couldn't speak a word of English six weeks earlier failed to pronounce his name correctly.

Astonishing.

What's also astonishing is that the story of the interaction never made it to the mainstream press. It wasn't shown on the main ITV network either. It was like it never happened. The video has also disappeared. Only those who saw it can recall it. What a shame, it was classic TV. And another example of jealousy from other ITV regions.

A few years later, I was at the City Ground for The Match and Emlyn Hughes was my guest. After the final whistle, we went downstairs and Cloughie invited us in for a drink.

"Oi Welsby. I hear you can take me off."

I'd done a dinner in Derby a couple of months earlier. Someone must have told him.

"Well go on then!!"

A bit unnerved, I went into my Cloughie with a gag.

"What's the difference between a Leeds United fan and a Jehovah's Witness?
When a Leeds United fan knocks on the door, he tells YOU to fuck off!"

Cloughie, who hated Leeds, pissed himself laughing.

"Great joke. Do it again!"

So I did.

"You're better doing me than Mike fucking Yarwood."

He was joking, but that was the most "relaxed" I'd ever seen him.

A general perception of Cloughie was that of a loudmouth who spoke his mind and didn't give a toss if anyone was offended. Part of that is true, but he was also a very studious man with a wonderful vocabulary. When speaking, he was extremely articulate. If in mid-flow and he needed a second's thinking time he'd say "that type of thing".

We all do it in different ways. It's momentary and enables you to weigh up what you're going to say next. It's involuntary and you don't even realise you've said it. And it was barely noticeable to whom he was talking to or to those just listening.

"That sort of thing."

In 1991, Brian showed a side of himself that was becoming more apparent. We were at the Baseball Ground for Derby County versus Tottenham Hotspur.

A couple of hours or so before kick-off, we received a phone call telling us that Brian was "ill" and wouldn't be able to come.

We knew the real reason.

Executive producer Trevor East was to the point. In so many words he explained if Brian didn't turn up, and the press asked us why, we'd tell them.

Trevor's threat was taken seriously. Cloughie arrived not long after and sat next to me. He certainly made his mark.

"Hey yer look nervous. Don't be nervous young man."

He started to sing.

"Yer make me feel so young – COME ON!"

So I joined in.

"You make me feel like Spring has sprung
And every time I see you grin
I'm such a happy individual"

This was 30 seconds before going on air and we were singing a duet! How many people can say they sang a duet with Tony Bennett and Brian Clough?

As the music started to fade from the opening titles of The Match, I was in the zone.

So I began my opening:

"And good afternoon from the Baseball Ground. No Gazza today of course, which is disappointing but we're more than compensated by a line-up that includes Gary Lineker, Dean Saunders, Peter Shilton Mark Wright and the World's number-one Granddad."

The camera cut to a badge on the blazer of my guest, saying "World's number-one Granddad", as I continued my introduction:

"Our special studio guest this afternoon, Brian Clough."

Cloughie thanked me but tripped over his words. He then proclaimed that his time at Derby was the happiest of his career. He was still boss of Derby's rivals Nottingham Forest. That can't have gone down well. He took Forest to the title, two European Cups and four League Cups!

We then discussed the situation with Derby being up for sale and Clough held back on his feelings. I think he contemplated going off on one. He'd previously criticised the owner Robert Maxwell. He resisted this time. With seconds to go before kick-off, he did make sure he got some last words in:

"I was talking to Brian Moore yesterday, who is possibly the best commentator and presenter in the business on your network. I don't mean that rudely of course. I said if there was a match for your network to pick, this is a good one."

He started to raise his voice.

"Venables. Cox. ME. YOU. LINEKER. SAUNDERS. What more can you have on a Sunday afternoon?"

I tried to keep a straight face. It was time for me to pass over to the match commentator.

"Brian Moore isn't here today. Our commentator is Alan Parry and Trevor Francis is with him."

Alan always had a good sense of humour and was ready with a reply:

"Thank you, Elton. Thanks Brian, I'm a big fan of yours as well."

During the first half, Cloughie left me and went for some fresh air. Right in the middle of the supporters!!

He returned for half-time analysis and the second half. Now back in place, Alan Parry threw to him so Cloughie could share his thoughts. He gave a generic response. Nothing memorable.

Parry continued his commentary. But Cloughie hadn't finished.

He turned to me.

"I've got something else to say."

I had to get the message to Alan Parry but via two outside broadcast trucks. They had to alert Alan that Brian had something to add. The whole process took about two minutes. The ball went out of play, giving Alan the chance to bring Cloughie back in.

"Well Brian, I believe you want to say something more."

"I've forgotten what it is."

The press picked up on something Cloughie DID say during the broadcast. A Gary Lineker goal had given Spurs a 1-0 win but Peter Shilton was at fault. Cloughie questioned the veteran keeper.

"Shilton's Shot It" was one of the headlines the next day – a direct quote from Cloughie.

After the game, I was chatting with the ITV team just outside the Baseball Ground, when a car drove past. Then it stopped. Brian got out of it. He came over to me, and shook my hand.

"Thank you, young man."

I think it was his way of showing appreciation for helping him get through it.

If I wasn't busy enough already, I had another offer on the table. I was doing a Superbowl event when The Doc and Steve Morrison approached me. They wanted to bring Kick Off back to Friday evenings.

My Saturdays and Sundays were already extremely busy, so I hesitated at the idea. I was also doing midweek highlights too.

I just couldn't let The Doc down. So I said yes.

My regular guest was John Bond, another huge mate of The Doc's. Bondy of course had managed Manchester City. He was a larger-than-life character. Bondy was never short of an opinion. We bounced off each other. I loved working with him. Wayne Garvie was still fairly new to the station, so he chaperoned Bondy when reporting outside of the studio.

One day they returned to Norwich, where John had managed. They took the train there. The camera crew got off beforehand so they could film Bondy leaving the train by himself. Like the return of the king. It made the whole segment look more impactful.

Bondie was outspoken. What he said didn't always go down well in certain quarters but we didn't care. It was good for the ratings.

On one occasion, he and Wayne went to Rochdale for a game against Burnley. Bondie had previously managed Burnley, and, according to the fans, not very well. At Spotland he was subjected to dogs' abuse.

Wayne was so concerned he phoned the Doc at home to tell him they were about to abort the mission for safety reasons. Doc agreed but also said "don't forget to test out the meat pies before you flee".

We had a running theme on Kick Off to rate the meat pies at all the grounds we visited. So on the way out, Bondie tasted a meat pie.

"Bootiful," was the verdict, in his distinctive accent.

Who came out on top of the "pie league" at the end of the season?

Wigan. Where else?

I've already mentioned Wayne in relation to the Bob Paisley 1983 tribute programme nearly going out when Bob died in 1996. Wayne worked his way up at Granada, and after Paul McDowell left, he was a great ally for the sports department. He's now a huge TV mogul in America. Wayne's done superbly well.

The return of Kick Off was a huge success. The viewing figures topped the one million mark. That's enormous for a regional show.

It should never have been taken off in the first place.

24

Hillsborough

This was always going to be a difficult chapter to do.

On Saturday 15th April 1989, Everton were at Villa Park to play Norwich City in one of the two FA Cup semi-finals taking place that day.

The other one was in South Yorkshire at Hillsborough, home of Sheffield Wednesday, between Nottingham Forest and Liverpool. As usual I was in London, doing the football results service.

It proved to be my most challenging situation on live television.

When I left home, one of the last things I knew was that my son Chris would be going to Hillsborough with his friend and their family. Chris is a Blue, the same as me. He was eleven years old at the time.

I was sat in the studio when both games began. My interest was concentrated on Villa Park of course. Very quickly, news came from Hillsborough. The referee had had to stop the game and take the players off. Some supporters were on the pitch.

As this was 1989, I'm sure many people thought it was crowd trouble. We'd become so used to it. The news continued to filter through. It became apparent that this was nothing to do with hooliganism. There was a real problem. And it was at the end where the Liverpool fans were.

I had to go on air. The game had been abandoned. A lot of different information was coming through. By the time I was live on ITV, we knew that people had died. As I read out the scores, the death toll mounted. It was just a blur.

Everton had won. It was irrelevant. I needed to know about my son. The moment the credits rolled on the results service, I ran to a phone to call home.

Chris wasn't at Hillsborough, as it turned out. He decided to play golf instead.

Football was in mourning. Fans from all over paid their respects. The city of Liverpool united in its grief. Kenny Dalglish led the club magnificently. Who could ever forget the way he summed up the floral tributes at Anfield.

"I've never seen anything more beautiful or so tragic."

Wow.

He offered words of comfort to bereaved families and helped his players do the same. Kenny and Marina, his wife, were admired by everyone on Merseyside for the way they orchestrated the club's response to that terrible, terrible day. The players, too, were outstanding. Footballers didn't train for this type of thing. They became counsellors. Astonishing, when you think of it.

Next up on The Match was a Merseyside Derby. The game was almost immaterial. In the presentation studio, I was joined by Craig Johnston who'd flown over from Australia to play his part in the grieving process. Craig spoke with so much feeling as red and blue scarves, tied together, were paraded around Goodison Park.

It was beautiful. It was tragic.

After the match, which ended goalless, Jim Rosenthal did a very poignant interview with Steve McMahon. The whole night captured the mood and spirit of Merseyside.

The city had been dealt an unprecedented and irreparable blow. The nation saw a remarkable unity through the keyhole of The Match that night.

25

Up for grabs

The 1988/89 season was heading to a dramatic finale. A season that will never be forgotten because of the tragedy of what happened on Saturday 15th April 1989. I still don't know how the Liverpool players and supporters were able to find the strength to finish the season. The emotional toll on everyone at the club was enormous. But here they were, heading for a league and cup double again.

It was fitting that the FA Cup final was between the two Merseyside clubs. The city was united in grief. The Blues stood side by side with the Reds. This was more than football. Now 1,000s upon 1,000s from the area headed to Wembley for the final. It was always going to be a difficult day.

Liverpool's 3-2 extra-time victory gave their fans some silverware to celebrate, as Evertonians set off back north. In the league, Liverpool still had two matches to play. Both at Anfield.

Firstly, they took on relegation-threatened West Ham. This was their game in hand over Arsenal, who were top by virtue of goals scored. The goal difference between the Gunners and Liverpool was identical.

A huge 5-1 win put the Reds in pole position and sent the Hammers down. But this is where things get even more interesting. Liverpool's final match of the season, set for the Friday night, was against Arsenal. Liverpool now held a three-point lead and a superior goal difference. Arsenal had to win the game by a minimum of two clear goals. If they did so, the title would go to North London based on the Gunners scoring more over the season.

The problem was that Liverpool rarely lost at home. And if they did, it was not by two goals or more. The league and cup double seemed to be in the bag for the Reds.

Did anyone give Arsenal a chance?

Friday 26th May arrived. ITV were covering it live. This was going to be some night at Anfield. Little did I know that the greatest ever climax to a season was about to unfold in front of my eyes.

In the early afternoon, I went to interview George Graham as part of the menu. He began with the usual stuff. "We're underdogs, we'll give it our best etc." It was pretty standard and nothing out of the ordinary. Then as we came towards the end, what he said gave me goosebumps.

"I'll tell yer what. If we score one, we'll score two."

I ended the interview immediately. It was the perfect way to finish. I thanked George. I knew he'd given me something special. The rest of the country may have written off Arsenal's chances, but their manager didn't think it was impossible.

I was really pleased with the interview and thought that George's words might make people at home pause and think for a minute. I still didn't believe Arsenal would do it, but George had planted a seed. Maybe they could.

When the interview was shown, they had cut George's line. It was ridiculous.

I arrived at Anfield nice and early and there was an air of expectation around the place. I saw the usual faces. Everyone I bumped into who was associated with Liverpool appeared confident. They'd seen their club dominate for so long. They weren't being arrogant, they just trusted their team. Despite Arsenal pushing them hard, Liverpool had been here before. More often than not, they came out on top.

With the excitement building, we did a live Kick Off show for the Granada region, with John Bond. George Graham's words from before were still in my mind. It's a shame that nobody got to see them. Once I finished with Bondy, I had to concentrate on being ready for the match itself.

Was something enormous about to happen?

The Kop were warming up. The scene was set.

I was counted in.

"5-4-3-2-1."

We were live!

I have to address a myth at this point too. It's been said that my guest that day on ITV wasn't scheduled to be Bobby Robson. As I recall, he was always booked to be on. Nobody else. I knew about Bobby being with me beforehand. Bobby was just perfect. He was the England manager at the time. And this was the biggest game in English football for a very long time.

Everything that you can imagine and have heard about Bobby is true. He later became Sir Bobby of course. He was a wonderful person, respectful, warm and polite. There was a delayed kick-off but that presented no problems. It gave me more time to speak with Bobby. Then I passed over to commentator Brian Moore.

The waiting was almost over.

Bobby and I watched the match together, with Ian St. John stationed slightly behind us on a stool. I have no idea why Saint chose that spot. He could've gone anywhere he wanted. But he chose there.

The game was very tense. But when Alan Smith put Arsenal ahead early in the second half, the Gunners only needed one more to do it. The tension and drama increased with every attack they had.

The moment that settled the season came in injury time. Brian Moore's commentary deserves the iconic status that it has.

"For Thomas. Charging through the midfield! THOMAS!

IT'S UP FOR GRABS NOW!

THOMAS!!! RIGHT AT THE END!"

Michael Thomas, through on goal, prodded the ball over Bruce Grobbelaar.

2-0 to Arsenal!!

They'd done it! With seconds left, Arsenal were the league champions.

The Saint was in shock. He put his head in his hands. And then fell backwards off of his stool!

At the same time, Bobby sat there shaking his head. He couldn't take it in either.

"This game never ceases to amaze me."

Bobby kept repeating himself.

"This game never ceases to amaze me."

He was mumbling.

"This game never ceases to amaze me."

It would have been great to talk more with Bobby on air, but because of the delayed kick-off, time was limited. Also, we couldn't delay News at Ten. Jim Rosenthal was able to interview some of the understandably ecstatic Arsenal players.

As Tony Adams was presented with the trophy, my thoughts went back to my interview with George Graham earlier that afternoon and his closing line.

"I'll tell yer what. If we score one, we'll score two."

Winning the league didn't give Arsenal a place in the European Cup though. The ban on English clubs was still in force, so the Gunners couldn't represent England overseas on the continent.

So they went to America instead.

On Sunday 6th August, just thirteen days before the start of the new season, Arsenal were in Florida to take on Independiente, the reigning champions of Argentina. It was seen by some as an unofficial World Club Championship. In truth, it was a pre-season friendly and the chance for the Arsenal lads to have a nice trip before defending their title.

The venue was the Joe Robbie Stadium, the then home of the Miami Dolphins. ITV decided to show the match live, but only in certain regions. The Doc, on behalf of Granada, didn't take it. With the time difference, it didn't come on until after News at Ten.

The Arsenal lads were still on a high after Anfield. Being at West Palm Beach with them didn't feel like work. We ate in great restaurants, we played golf and we had more than a few drinks. It was roasting hot as well. I remember thinking to myself that this was money for old rope.

One day I played golf with Niall Quinn and Theo Foley. Quinny took the money, 20 dollars. The idea was that it would go behind the bar after we'd changed. In the time it took to finish the round and go to the bar, Quinny had lost it!

The game itself was a farce. The referee lost control quickly and yellow cards were brandished at will. Players were getting some bad knocks. Both sides were squaring up to each other. It was far from friendly.

Even Arsenal physio Gary Lewin was sent off. He only came on the field to get some water to the players. Gary was distraught. He just wanted to help. The temperature was at boiling point. He feared a ban when he got back to England.

A representative from the Football League was there and I told him what state Lewin was in. The poor fella was heartbroken. The league official told me that he saw everything and it was much ado about nothing. I went to see Gary in the dressing room and passed on the message. He was so relieved and the colour started to come back into his face.

For those interested, two goals from David Rocastle gave Arsenal a 2-1 win and so they won the Zenith Data Systems Challenge Trophy. I don't know how many people actually cared.

The biggest irony is that we had over thirty minutes of time to fill after the final whistle. Back in May at Anfield, we had far less time. This time, when most people had switched off or fallen asleep with boredom, we had time to kill. What a shame. It wasn't easy to string things along either. We didn't have a great deal to talk about. Put it this way, I interviewed George Graham and David Dein. Twice!

That famous night on 26th May 1989 was without doubt one of the highlights of my career. People think I say that because I'm an Evertonian. That's ridiculous. They're wrong. It's because I witnessed football history being made. There's never been a more dramatic finale to an English top-flight season.

I know the Manchester City 2012 title win is considered to be special, but the context is totally different. 1989 was a straight shoot-out between the top two. I'm not taking anything away from City. But QPR weren't at the same level. They went down to ten men too. City were the clear favourites to win. Once QPR realised they were safe from relegation, they took their foot off the gas.

Liverpool versus Arsenal battling for the league, with the odds against the away side, will always be the number one for me. It's the greatest night in English domestic football. And remains so to this day.

26

Italia 90

The 1990 World Cup in Italy is seen as the moment where modern football began. A whole generation of new football fans fell in love with the game. Many people get nostalgic about the tournament. England's run to the semi-finals certainly helped.

We normally did everything from England. The traditional way. A presenter with a panel from a studio in London. This time, we decided to use another approach. We were still going to have people back home. However, the new idea was to be live at the World Cup from the stadium itself.

I was going to be the main presenter in Italy, which was exciting. There would only be place for me and one guest. Space was limited. We were going to be right in the middle of the fans. It'd never been done before. There was one major concern about this assignment though. Being among the supporters, I'd have great difficulty hearing my producer and the PA.

So before heading off for Italy, I visited a hearing aid shop in Liverpool. They made me a special earpiece, which was melted and moulded into my ear. It blocked out all outside noise.

Prior to the big kick-off, there wasn't much optimism about England's chances. Scotland and Ireland had also qualified. The first match was between the holders Argentina and Cameroon in the San Siro stadium, in Milan. ITV had this opening game. I was joined by Trevor Francis, who had represented England many times and also played in Italy.

Very quickly, I realised my new earpiece was just the job. Back home, the stadium must have looked incredible. But there'd been an enormous storm and the pitch was in a right mess. Argentina were not happy about it. It looked practically unplayable. The match was never going to be postponed though. That would've been too embarrassing for the hosts and FIFA.

When London came to Trevor and I, we broke the news about the playing surface. In fact, they'd only finished laying it the day before. The torrential rain had made it into a quagmire and there were visible holes in the turf.

It was awful.

Not the best way to start the World Cup.

Before kick-off, I heard a conversation in my ear between Jeff Farmer and Phil King, who were outside the San Siro in one of our trucks.

"If this doesn't work, we'll do everything from London."

That pissed me off.

What I didn't know, is that the links were crashing. That meant that when I cued in a video clip, like Jim Rosenthal with the England camp, the timing was wrong.

From London, I heard:

"If Elton can't handle it, we'll have to scrap it."

Strange. I never crashed links.

Jean Wallace, the Doc's future wife, was the production assistant (PA) out in Italy. And she was the only person that figured it all out. There was a time delay. I was still speaking when the studio cut to the next VT (video tape). During the count from London, Jean did the maths and solved the problem which threatened to bring our tournament to a premature end. This isn't meant as a pun, but I'm going to take a brief "timeout" to explain the role of a PA in a live TV broadcast.

One night Jean was asked to be PA on News at Ten. A programme timed to the last second. ITN's top newsreader of the day was the presenter. Towards the end, Jean calculated that the programme was going to finish ten seconds early.

She told the producer that the newsreader needed to ad lib for ten seconds at the end.

"He doesn't ad lib."

Jean was shocked as she was so used to live sport, where having to fill in for ten seconds is par for the course. Somehow by picking up a couple of seconds here and there they arrived on time for the newsreader's eight seconds closing link.

That's how precise live television is.

The working relationship between the presenter and the PA is closer and more important than the presenter and the director. Presenters need to know the time available during every part of a programme. That's the PA's responsibility, to get the time absolutely spot on. A half-hour programme, like Kick Off, would last for say 27 minutes and 17 seconds. The PA's precision is absolutely vital to a live programme finishing to the second.

Back to the San Siro.

Cameroon's 1-0 win over Argentina was a huge shock. Did the terrible pitch play a part? When you have artists like Diego Maradona in your team, you can't expect them to perform on something like that.

There was a drawback at being at so many different games. The amount of miles we had to cover. We were christened "The Travelling Wilburys". We used planes, trains and automobiles to get around Italy. Despite going to some wonderful cities like Turin and Milan, we hardly saw them. It was an exhausting schedule.

Rodney Marsh was a great "Wilbury". He was never bothered about the amount of travelling we did; he managed it easily. He was always good for morale and lifting our tired spirits. When we arrived at one of the airports, Rod collected a load of Italian lira off everyone. The first person to get their suitcase off the carousel won the cash. It was about 50,000 lira.

Probably about a tenner back then!

Palermo was an interesting place. It was one of the very few cities where I managed to have a look around. I was with Nick Beaumont and we had itchy feet. Rod had gone for a sleep, so with time on our hands, Nick and I decided to leave the hotel.

Palermo is considered the birthplace of the mafia.

So we asked our interpreter Enzo if it was safe to go.

"You see the lights down there? When you reach them, turn left. Do not under any circumstances turn right."

So left it was.

Rod was my live guest when West Germany played UAE during the group stages. Yet another storm hit Milan. What happened next was crazy. The ITV van was struck by lightning and we both got an electric shock live on air. Can you imagine if it'd been more powerful? Rod and I would've been fried to death live on television!

That's one way to get the TV ratings up I suppose!

After being with Ireland at Euro 88 and my friendship with Jack Charlton, I was rooting for them as well. When they got through the group stages, I was in Genoa for their knockout match against Romania.

I was in with the fans again, alongside Ian St. John. With our connections to Jack, we badly wanted the Irish to win. Their game with the Romanians was forgettable until it had to be decided by a penalty shootout.

Then the drama began.

At 4-4, goalkeeper Packie Bonner saved the fifth Romanian penalty. If Ireland scored, they'd be into the quarter-finals. We looked to see who the taker was. Substitute David O'Leary stepped forward.

Sorry David, but both Saint and I shouted "Oh shit!" in unison.

We'd never seen O'Leary take a penalty before. I'd done plenty of research and had no record of him taking one. O'Leary had also fallen out of favour with Big Jack too. His crime? David O'Leary was a ball-playing defender, who liked to pass to feet and play out from the back. That went against Jack's philosophy.

A nation held its breath. It was truly a tense moment.

HE SCORES!!

It was never in doubt!

Saint and I celebrated as if we were Irish. O'Leary's penalty was perfect and Ireland were through. I had a great sleep that night.

It might have been down to bumping into a jubilant Liam Brady after the match. Liam played for Sampdoria in the 1980s and knew Genoa well. He offered to take me out. Liam took me to a really good night spot on the beach. We had to take our shoes off and wade through water before we could even order a drink.

The following Saturday, Ireland lost narrowly to Italy by a single goal scored by the eventual Golden Boot winner, Toto Schillaci.

Before the tournament began, Aston Villa had given the FA permission to speak with Graham Taylor, who'd just taken Villa to second place. Graham was chosen ahead of Howard Kendall, Terry Venables and Howard Wilkinson to succeed Bobby Robson as the England boss. The new manager would take over after the World Cup.

Graham became my sidekick in Italy. He was really coy about his new role though. He certainly didn't want to discuss it on air. Privately, he was very open about his plans for the future. When he came out to Italy, I got to know him well.

A week before the final, Joyce and the kids had flown out. So with Graham in tow, we all used to go out for dinner. We were in a lovely restaurant one night, seated fairly close to the kitchen. The serving hatch was just behind Chris, who was tucking into a melon and ham. All of a sudden, the hatch crashed opened and hit Chris on the back of his head. He went face first into the melon!

SQUELCH!!

I thought Graham was going to wet himself, as poor Chris tried to wipe all the mushed fruit off his face.

I got to spend a fair bit of time with Graham Taylor. I had his trust and we talked for hours.

Graham was a big fan of Nigel Clough. He shared with me that he wanted to build his new England side around Nigel. Graham had a clear vision. He also wanted Joe Royle involved to run the under 21s along with Lawrie McMenemy. Graham asked me about Joe, as I'd known him for years. I rang Joe from Italy and passed Taylor over to him. Then I left them to it.

We also socialised with the likes of Helen Francis, wife of Trevor and Michelle Lineker. They taught Laura to swim. I didn't see the England players, nor Bobby Robson.

Such was the life of a Travelling Wilbury.

27

None shall sleep

There were four players that I considered to be part of a unique group. The best of all time. Pelé, Cruyff, Best and Maradona. I'd already met three out of the four. There was one that I hadn't met.

Chris and I were heading to a lift at the end of the corridor. There was another guy waiting by the doors.

I looked at Chris.

"Is that who I think it is?"

He nodded.

The doors opened and the three of us got in.

We were sharing a lift with Pelé!

We shook hands and had an all too brief conversation. Then just like that, the journey was over. But I'd completed the set.

It was only recently that I told the story to the youngest of my two grandsons, Oscar. He didn't believe me.

"You met Pelé? Really Granddad?"

To Oscar, aged only nine, Pelé is the greatest of all time. He loves what Maradona could do with a ball, but Pelé is his hero.

In Italy though, there was one place where Diego was God. Naples.

The first semi-final between Italy and Argentina was there. That meant Maradona playing for his country in the city where he was adored. He'd helped changed Napoli's fortunes. They won the league twice and the UEFA Cup with him. They still idolise him there today. It also meant that there was the strange matter of some of the locals supporting Argentina simply because of Maradona. That created a tense atmosphere.

We arrived in Naples the day before. Our hotel had a superb view of the fort – a structure right on the front. This was another rare occasion where had some time to explore a little. Yet again, Nick Beaumont was a willing companion. We wanted to see the authentic part of the city. Away from the tourist traps. The real backstreets.

We were out for around two hours, going up and down these winding streets. We dropped into the odd bar for a drink. If we wanted to turn right, we turned right. When we decided to go left, we went left. We didn't ask Enzo for advice. We observed the local culture. It was fascinating.

We arrived back at the hotel to find an amateur operatic evening going on. We listened to it for a bit. Afterwards we met the main tenor, who spoke excellent English.

"Are you having a good time? What have you been doing?"

"Well, we left the hotel and wandered round the backstreets over there. It was wonderful."

The tenor's face turned to one of horror.

"What??"

"Yeah, we popped into a couple of places, had a few drinks."

"You can't go there! Nobody goes there!"

"Why not?"

"It's Camorra country!"

Camorra is the mafia in Naples. Nick and I had a lucky escape.

The next day, we decided to get some air and leave the hotel. The traffic was so busy. It was impossible to cross the road. We waited at a set of traffic lights for about five minutes. The locals just ignored them.

The tenor from the opera was leaving at the same time as us.

"What are you doing?"

"We're trying to cross the road but nobody is stopping to let us."

"You don't do that here, watch me."

He walked out into the middle of the traffic. Cars were having to break for him. Nick and I looked at each other and quickly followed. It took some bottle I can tell you. It was madness. Most of the cars were scratched or had big bumps on them. Road rage was commonplace.

When we got back to the hotel, Steve Coppell had arrived with Wayne Garvie. Steve had no accommodation booked, so he bunked in with me.

One rule was in force in Naples; no alcohol. For twenty-four hours, nowhere was allowed to serve any type of booze. One of our cameramen found that hard to believe. Off he went, determined to find the only place in Naples where we could have a proper drink. About one hour later, he returned with a spring in his step. He'd found a lovely restaurant that was only one hundred yards from the hotel.

"I've scored! I told them who we were and who we were representing. I've booked a table for midnight."

He'd asked them about the alcohol ban. He'd been assured not to worry.

We did the game. It wasn't a classic. As expected, the atmosphere was strange because of the Naples/Maradona factor. Italy went out on penalties, so it was very subdued on the return to the hotel.

Our group met up, ready to go to the restaurant. It's fair to say we were a little excited about the thought of unwinding with a few glasses of wine. We followed the cameraman. We couldn't believe how close it was to the hotel.

On arrival, we were greeted by the maître d'.

Picture Marlon Brando in The Godfather. He was a dead ringer.

"Welcome, welcome. I serve you tonight."

"Thank you, what's your name?"

"I'm Mario."

"I'm Elton."

There was only our group of 12 in there. Mario came and took everyone's orders. He got to me.

"Mr Elton, what would you like?"

"I'll have what you would have."

He put his hands around my face. And kissed me on both cheeks.

Mario's choice was spaghetti alle vongole, a Neapolitan dish. It was magnificent. I've tried it elsewhere since. I've never had one as good as that night. Mario didn't just bring the food. He served us beer and wine. Heaven!

Then two other people arrived.

The Carabinieri.

In other words, the police.

They'd looked through the window and seen us sat there with our drinks on the table.

Oh shit!

Mario went over to them and had an animated conversation. There was a lot of gesticulating. The two policemen were visibly sweating. Then they turned round, left the restaurant and drove off.

I'd nearly finished my spaghetti so I got up from the table.

"Everything alright Mario? What was the problem?"

"No, no, no, Mr Elton. No problem. I just explained to them. Our power, is greater than theirs."

Camorra.

Not long after, we thanked Mario and left for our hotel. We were tired. It'd been a gruelling day and we'd had a few at the restaurant. By about 2 am, I was in bed.

At 4.20 am, Naples was invaded!

Steve and I thought World War III had begun. Loud bangs were followed by flashes of light. We shit ourselves. We had no idea what the hell was happening. Steve and I leapt out of bed and ran to the window.

There was a huge fireworks display.

At 4.20 am!!!

It had been planned to coincide with Italy reaching the final. Of course, with Argentina winning, the display never happened. Someone, in their infinite wisdom, decided it would be a good idea to go ahead anyway and do it in the middle of the night.

We were exhausted. We had to be in Turin within a few hours for the other semi-final between England and West Germany. The two cities weren't even close to each other. No wonder we were called The Wilburys.

After freshening up at yet another hotel, we went to the stadium for the big one. Nobody expected England to get this far. The match was being shown live on both ITV and BBC1. Graham Taylor was alongside me. Next to us was the World Cup winning captain Bobby Moore with Jonathan Pearce of Capital Radio.

I went over to Bobby, who I'd never met before. I introduced myself and asked him if he'd appear for the opening with

Graham Taylor and myself. A few moments later, we went live and I introduced our unscheduled guest.

Not too far away, Des Lynam was there for the BBC. They'd decided to try and emulate ITV by presenting from the ground. Des had difficulty communicating with London because he didn't have an earpiece like mine. He never stood a chance.

The fact that you're reading this book means I can safely assume you know what happened in the semi-final between England and West Germany. I don't need to tell you. Out in Turin, we were all as disappointed as everyone back home. The lasting memory was Gazza crying.

Sunday 8th July 1990 arrived.

Before the final, England were announced as winners of the FIFA Fair Play award. We interviewed Gary Lineker in the stadium just before he and Bobby Robson were presented with it. After finishing the segment, Gary climbed down over rows and rows of seats to join Bobby. It was a long way.

He reached the pitch, then he stopped and climbed back over the seats to come back up to us.

"Don't forget, I've never been booked in my career."

It was all very odd. He'd gone out of his way just to tell me something that I already knew. In fairness to Gary, it was appropriate.

I took Chris to the game but I couldn't stay with him because I was working. A mate of Doc's, Des Windsor agreed to look after him. The final itself was dreadful. Probably the worst ever. We saw a lot of the dark side of football. Cynical fouls, time wasting and diving. A horrible event. West Germany won 1-0.

I was glad it was over.

Afterwards, everyone met up to catch a bus that had been organised for us. Not just the crew but also the ITV dignitaries. Doc was there, and so was Des Windsor.

"Where's our Chris?"

"I don't know."

Chris was twelve years old at the time. I ran around the stadium, trying to find my son. It was so hot and humid. There were people everywhere. I did a full lap of the Olympic Stadium. He was nowhere to be seen.

I got back to the bus, I was frantic with worry. Then I looked up. There was Chris, walking towards us, hand in hand with Helen Francis and Michelle Lineker.

What a relief!

We flew home the very next day.

Arrivederci Italia.

28

The perfect match

As the new decade continued, I was as busy as ever. The World Cup was over but it was business as usual when the new football season began. I had Kick Off on Friday nights up in Manchester and midweek highlights too. Then it was down to London for the results service. And of course, the live games would restart on Sundays too.

I loved every minute of it!

There was also a major difference when the first matches kicked off that Saturday afternoon.

It was still only just over a year since Hillsborough, but England's run to the semi-finals at Italia 90 had introduced the game to more people.

One player epitomised it all.

Paul Gascoigne.

Gazzamania was sweeping the nation. The Tottenham midfielder had captured the hearts of the English fans. It wasn't just his performances either. His tears after realising he would be suspended for the final struck a chord with many. The general public had their new working-class hero.

It was going to be hard for Paul to cope with all the fame. He was still only 23 years old.

When 1991 arrived, we were at White Hart Lane to do Spurs against Manchester United. The match had one memorable moment. And it was Gazza who stole the headlines.

For the wrong reasons.

In the second half, he was sure that Gary Lineker had been fouled in the box. So Gascoigne decided to let the referee

Vic Callow know about it. We were showing the replay of the alleged penalty incident while the protests continued. It was a nothing challenge and never a penalty. We cut back just in time to see Callow show a straight red card to Gazza for talking out of turn.

Once the game was done, we were in the club lounge when Paul collared me. He was still upset about the sending off.

"Elton, can yee help me oot? I didnae do nowt."

Gazza was adamant that he was innocent and thought we could clear his name.

"Sorry Paul, but the cameras didn't catch anything. There's nothing I can do."

He was really down about it but we had no evidence to back him up. The pressure was getting to him by this point. Everyone wanted a piece of Gazza.

Five months later, with a transfer to Lazio in Italy already organised, Paul Gascoigne had a public meltdown during the FA Cup final win over Nottingham Forest. He should've already been sent off for a terrible tackle on Garry Parker. Shortly after, he scythed down Gary Charles. Cloughie was fuming, believing that Gascoigne should've been sent off twice.

The impact from his lunge on Charles left Gazza badly injured. Paul left the field on a stretcher and never played for Tottenham again. Many years later, referee Roger Milford admitted that he should have shown Gazza a red card. Milford also said that he felt sorry for him. Like rubbing salt in Cloughie's wounds.

In the early days of covering The Match, Paul had been a guest with me as his old club Newcastle United took on Manchester United. His cheekiness was for there all to see as well. And he continued it after the final whistle.

We were positioned in a part of St. James' Park that at best could be described as unsteady. It was a box on top of some scaffolding. It wasn't very elegant or sturdy. Once the game ended, we were ready to go.

We were high up above the Manchester United supporters. They often serenaded me when I was presenting at Old Trafford.

"Elton Welsby, you're a whacker, you're a whacker!"

At least that's what I think they were saying.

This time they turned their attention to Gazza. As soon as they saw him, they kicked off. Nothing too malicious, just typical terrace chanting. Paul decided to react, with a few hand gestures of his own and stuck his tongue out, as he often did.

Paul didn't care. He lapped it up. Gazza thought it was funny and they were fair game because they started it. I was more concerned that one crackpot might take it a little too far.

Thankfully we got away unscathed.

One man who could sympathise with Gazza was the original football superstar; George Best. When I was still a kid, through my dad's work we sometimes got tickets to Old Trafford. We only went for one reason. To watch George Best.

Despite his playing career being over, people were still fascinated with Bestie. I was delighted when, from time to time, he joined me as a guest on The Match. I have to say I was always in awe of him.

It wasn't always plain sailing though. We were at Highbury one Sunday afternoon and George arrived looking a little fragile. Producer Trevor East had clocked on to this.

"Ask him what he had for breakfast!"

"What?"

"Ask George what he had for breakfast!"

So I did.

Bestie slurred his reply. He had to be replaced. I was friendly with George and I didn't want to see him like this. Bobby Robson, who was also at the game, stepped in at the last minute.

Bestie was also booked for a match at the City Ground between Nottingham Forest and Liverpool. It was on New Year's Day. Not the ideal choice, following the booziest night of the year. But he was fine. I was relieved. He arrived for another game once and he was stone cold sober. Except he had a big black eye! The make-up department did wonders that day. Nobody could tell.

Bestie couldn't say no. He got a reputation for not turning up for things, but it's because he'd say yes to everyone. More often than not, he was double-booked or even triple-booked.

One day, I was with him, Rodney Marsh and The Doc in Manchester. Rod and Bestie went way back and had been mates for years. I knew Marshie well and of course he'd been with me in Italy for the World Cup. We were in an Italian restaurant, with two women sat behind us. They weren't exactly blessed with good looks.

Before we knew it, Bestie was up and over talking to them. It wasn't long after that, the three of them left.

George turned to us and laughed:

"Well someone's got to."

Manchester United fans still sing about Bestie today. There's a statue of him alongside Sir Bobby Charlton and Denis Law at Old Trafford. At Everton, we've our Holy Trinity of Kendall, Ball and Harvey. United have Law, Best and Charlton.

Of course, Denis Law was someone that I'd known well for years through our time together on Kick Off. In 1991, when United got to the European Cup Winners' Cup final, ITV invited Denis to be part of the team.

UEFA had finally lifted their ban on English clubs in Europe after the Heysel tragedy in 1985. In the first season back, Manchester United had made it to the final. The match against Barcelona was in Rotterdam. The memories came flooding back to me. We were in the same stadium where Everton lifted the trophy after victory over Rapid Vienna in 1985.

Our other guest for the 1991 final was Jimmy Greaves. By now, Greavsie was a national treasure. He'd fought alcoholism to become a popular TV personality. He didn't just do Saint and Greavsie, he was a regular co-commentator for us and also appeared on breakfast TV.

Before we went on air, I was stood talking to Denis and Jimmy. For a second, I looked at them both and thought back to when I was a young lad at Goodison Park. The two greatest goal scorers of my youth. Now they were stood next to me, ready to go live to the nation. I had to pinch myself.

Good work if you can get it.

Denis was revered wherever he went. He was at the City Ground once and Cloughie dragged him into the dressing room and introduced him to the Forest players:

"Gentlemen, this man is the greatest. Even better than me!"

Johan Cruyff was the coach of Barcelona and his side were favourites. But United beat Barcelona 2-1 that night. Alex Ferguson had won his second trophy at the club.

I was happy for Denis, for Fergie and also for Mark Hughes who scored United's two goals. After leaving Old Trafford in 1986, he'd endured a frustrating time at Barcelona. After a year on loan at Bayern Munich, Mark rejoined United in 1988.

Now "Sparky" returned to haunt his old club.

Mark was a guest a few times on Granada Soccer Night and we had an excellent rapport.

Alex Ferguson was close to The Doc. Paul helped him handle the media and Fergie didn't forget those who were on his side. When he took the Manchester United job, he inherited a mess. I was sent to interview Alex before his very first game as manager in November 1986, away to Oxford United. I was staying in the same hotel as the team, and when I was in the bar I bumped into an old pal.

Physio Jimmy McGregor was still at United, he hadn't left with Ron or his assistant Mick Brown. You already know how far back me and Jimmy go, firstly through Everton and also Northern Ireland.

I went over and introduced myself to Alex. He was about to start a game of snooker with Jimmy and kitman Norman Davies. Alex asked me if I wanted to make up the numbers, so they could play doubles. Fergie was relaxed and ready for the game the next day.

I did the interview early on the Saturday morning and then I had to take it back with me to London Weekend Television. My good friend Jim Ramsey needed time to edit it for the Saint and Greavsie show.

We always hear the story that Fergie would've been sacked in 1990 if United lost to Nottingham Forest in the 3rd round of the FA Cup. I was in London when I bumped into the club's chairman, Martin Edwards. We ended up having a night out together and we had a fair few. I asked him about the sacking story. He told me that he was never going to fire Fergie, no matter what happened that day at the City Ground.

That's what he told me and I believed him. He saw what Fergie was building behind the scenes. So did the board of directors, including Bobby Charlton. They backed him. And they won the lot.

That didn't happen immediately. There was still some heartache to come for Alex Ferguson.

None of us had any idea what was about to unfold.

29

The final season

The summer of 1991 was a fairly quiet affair with no international tournaments.

It's important to point out that we didn't broadcast a game every weekend. We were only allowed to show a limited number of fixtures. Viewers at home missed out on a lot. It wasn't like today when there are games all the time. Maybe it's too much. Less was certainly more back in 1991.

By Christmas, the top two had opened a gap between the rest. Manchester United and Leeds were neck and neck. Incredibly, Leeds were going to play United three times over the space of two weeks. On 29th December, we were there live for the league meeting. There was a fair bit of hype in the press, with the rivalry between the two clubs stoking up the atmosphere. It wasn't going to decide the title but it gave one side the chance to push ahead.

My guest was the Leeds legend, Big Jack.

He was in fine form before we went on air. But there was one slight concern for him. How to pronounce one of the names on the team sheet. Andrei Kanchelskis. Jack had been practising and he was getting the hang of it.

During the half-time analysis Jack highlighted a Kanchelskis run down the wing. And he nailed it! An absolutely perfect pronunciation of Andrei Kanchelskis!

Then he mentioned the Leeds goalie:

"John Loo-kick."

It was John Lukic by the way for those of you who weren't sure.

In January, Lee Chapman got injured. Manager Howard Wilkinson needed a solution. The weather was really cold around this time and some games were being called off.

Players were having to train inside to stay in shape. Sheffield Wednesday manager Trevor Francis saw this as an opportunity to invite a trialist to join them.

His name was Eric Cantona.

The Frenchman was having a bad time in his homeland and his career looked to be over in France. England appeared to be one escape route for the man labelled as the "enfant terrible" – the bad boy of French football.

After Cantona had spent a short time with Wednesday, Francis was still unsure what to do. He asked Cantona to extend his trial. Trevor told me himself that he wanted to see Eric on grass. He refused. It wasn't long before Wilkinson made a move. Cantona arrived at Leeds on an initial loan. He was an unknown quantity. But Wilkinson was prepared to gamble.

As the season headed towards the final straight, Manchester United and Leeds were still fighting for the title. Manchester United were also in the semi-finals of the League Cup. ITV invited Fergie to White Hart Lane for the second leg of the other semi, between Spurs and Nottingham Forest.

It was memorable to say the least.

Firstly, there was a bomb scare. An explosive device had been found close to the stadium and, of course, that meant the game was in doubt. Happily, everything was okay and the match went ahead after a long delay. Of course, to top it off, the semi-final went to extra time. Fergie and I had more talking to do.

Roy Keane scored to send Forest to Wembley, and both Alex and myself set off back to Manchester by plane after navigating through the capital. We sat together and made some small talk.

Then Fergie asked me a question that completely changed the conversation.

"You knew Bill Shankly didn't you?"

"Yes, I knew him fairly well. We were even colleagues for a time."

"What was he like?"

Alex had this incredible enthusiasm to learn more about Bill. I already knew how much he loved other great Scottish managers like Jock Stein and Sir Matt Busby. The time flew by and before we knew it, we were back in the North West. I really enjoyed reminiscing about Shanks to Alex. I think it helped create a closer bond between Fergie and I because our paths would cross a lot more.

Although Alex appeared relaxed on that flight home, within a couple of weeks the heat was on. Leeds were not going away and Manchester United were wobbling. With two games left, Leeds were away to Sheffield United with Manchester United going to Anfield for our live game. When Leeds won 3-2, it meant only one thing; if United lost to Liverpool, Leeds would be champions.

The Anfield crowd made a ferocious noise when the teams came out. The home supporters were relishing the thought of ending the hopes of their fierce rivals. Ian Rush, who up to this point had never scored against United throughout his career, chose this match to get his first. When Mark Walters added a second with just three minutes to go, it was over.

Leeds United were champions of England.

It was a remarkable story, and is largely forgotten about today. Why? It happened before the Premier League began.

We had cameras at Lee Chapman's house, where he was celebrating with some of his teammates including Cantona. Denis Law was my guest and we passed over live to congratulate them, as they squeezed together on Chapman's sofa.

I don't speak French, but I just had to say something to Eric Cantona.

"Magnifique Eric."

"You speak French?"

Denis replied:

"Un peu."

Old Trafford's King Denis and le Roi.

Alex Ferguson had the very small consolation of United winning their first League Cup. They'd beaten Forest in April. But the league title had evaded the club once more. The press debated if they'd ever win it again.

We didn't know it at the time, but that game at Anfield turned out to be the end of The Match.

When I look back at the four years of doing the live games, I do so with great pride. There were special moments. None more so than the title decider at Anfield in 1989. But there was more to it than that. I had so many different guests. That kept it fresh for the audience. It wasn't the same people each time, as is it today.

The unpredictable Cloughie, George Best, Andy Gray, Graham Taylor, Jimmy Greaves, Big Jack, Bobby Robson. And many others. We had variety and they were all characters in their own right, bringing something different to the coverage.

Over those four years, we travelled the length and breadth of the country. We visited most of the First Division grounds. Two chairmen were particularly hospitable. Bob Murray of Sunderland invited us to arrive early at Roker Park for an Easter lunch.

Brian Moore, Jimmy Greaves, Trevor East, Jeff Farmer and I were looked after in style. The boardroom looked splendid, but what about the grub? Well Bob had arranged for a bike rider to hurtle down from Whitley Bay with about a dozen portions of fish and chips. The best I've ever tasted as well!

It was freezing cold at Roker that day, but I was alright in a little studio equipped with a portable fan heater. Mooro and Greavsie were on the roof, wearing thermals, thick coats and ear muffs. Greavsie said he'd never been so cold. I waved at him from my cozy position. He just snarled and gestured. A bit like Harvey Smith!

Another ground where we were welcomed by the chairman was Villa Park.

I knew in advance. I got a phone call at home one Friday night. It was Doug Ellis. "Deadly Doug" as he was christened by Greavsie. He invited me to arrive early so he could show me recent developments at the ground and have a spot of lunch.

"With pleasure, Mr Chairman."

Needless to say, the guided tour took in all the ideas that were down to Doug. According to Doug anyway! He had an ego the size of an elephant, but he was harmless unless you happened to be his manager. He sacked eleven of them in his two terms as Villa chairman, hence his nickname "Deadly".

Doug himself, a keen angler, said the nickname came after a fishing trip with Greavsie. Jimmy was quite taken by the way Doug executed the fish he caught. So Greavsie christened him "Deadly Doug".

Yeah, sure!

After the match, I was back in the boardroom with Doug introducing to me to all his distinguished guests. One of them was the punk violinist, Nigel Kennedy. Quick as a flash, violin at the ready, he started playing the Match of the Day theme tune. Everyone thought it was hysterical.

I needed to get home.

"Anyway, thanks for your marvellous hospitality, Doug. I'm off."

"Give my love to Chester."

He knew I lived about 25 minutes away from there. So I was forced to sit back down as he told me about his childhood and schooling in Cheshire.

Think of a shy and retiring elderly chap. Then imagine the complete opposite.

Introducing "Deadly Doug" Ellis!

30

Euro 92

I didn't have long to get over the end of the domestic football season before turning my attention to Sweden. The country had been chosen to host Euro 92 and just as I'd been in Italy two years previously at the World Cup, I was going to be ITV's man in the stadium.

After the success of our coverage at Italia 90, the decision was made to do the games from the grounds. There would be no studio in London like in past years.

This was a first for English television.

Ireland manager and England World Cup winner Jack Charlton would be with me all the way. Jack was available because Ireland had narrowly missed out on qualification for the tournament. England advanced from that group instead. Scotland also made it to the Euros, meaning we had two British representatives.

There wasn't a lot of positivity about England's chances beforehand. Manager Graham Taylor's squad had been ravaged by injuries. Graham had also left some talented players like Chris Waddle and Peter Beardsley at home. Paul Gascoigne still hadn't recovered from his injury in the 1991 FA Cup final either.

Graham was under pressure. The press smelled blood.

There was also the intriguing story involving Denmark. War had broken out in Yugoslavia and so they weren't allowed to take part. The Danes replaced them. Some of the players were on holiday. In bars. On beaches. They'd now be the ultimate underdogs.

When we got to Sweden, we met up with Bryan King. Bryan was a former goalkeeper, who not only played for Coventry City and Millwall but also over in Scandinavia. Bryan still lived there and was married to a former Miss Sweden. She was stunning. Bryan was going to be our "Mr Fix-it".

We soon came to love the country. Big Jack of course was famously terrible at remembering names and butchering pronunciations. But when we visited Gothenburg, he insisted on pronouncing it like a local.

So from then on, Oo-ter-burg it was. Okay, he still had a North East twang when he said it, but he had it off to a tee.

Bryan was a cracking guide for us. He knew where to go and what to do, and he rolled out the red carpet for us. He organised a huge buffet for us one evening, after we'd spent some time earlier that day on the beach. It was more like a holiday than work at this point. Kingy had invited a load of his friends too.

I got talking to a couple of them and they invited me to a party back at their place. I tried to get Jack to come but he wanted to go back to the hotel. I decided to carry on the evening and set off with Kingy's mates to this party in the countryside. It was great and their hospitality was second to none.

It was perhaps a bit too good because the next thing I knew, I woke up in a hammock between two trees. I was in the middle of woodland, somewhere outside Oo-ter-burg. I had no idea where I was or how I got there either. I was fine but it was impossible to know what time it was. It was daylight almost all the time during this part of the year.

I managed to get my bearings and went back to the house where the party was. People were awake. Turned out it was around 8 am, so I had some breakfast and explained that I needed to get back to my hotel.

When I arrived, I saw Big Jack walking along the side of the river. He was looking down into the water. He would pause, then put his hand above his brow so he could see better. Jack was famous for his love of fishing. I thought he was checking out the river to see what he could catch later, so I called out to him:

"Hey Jack, anything biting?"

He turned round, quick as a flash.

"Fuckin' hell, I was looking for you!"

Jack thought I'd got pissed and fallen into the river! He was half-right!

Big Jack wasn't the only Charlton family member over in Sweden. Sir Bobby, Jack's younger brother was over there working for the BBC. There'd been rumours for a while that the two of them had fallen out.

When Jack talked about his brother to me, he called him "our Robert". Sometimes, it was "our kid". But when describing the player, he referred to him as Bobby Charlton. It was like they weren't related.

With both Charltons working in Sweden, the inevitable was bound to happen and their paths would cross. It had to be in Jack's new favourite place too: Göteborg.

We were in the stadium and I was glancing around, just taking it all in. In the tier below us, I spotted Bobby, eating a sandwich. I was so close to Jack by this point, so I simply told him that "your kid" is down there.

"Miserable bastard."

"Come on Jack, do me a favour, he's your brother. Life's too short. What if something happened to him? For God's sake, say hello."

Jack looked down at Bobby, who was still eating and decided to make the effort.

"Gizza bite!"

Bobby looked up. Then he looked down and carried on with his sandwich.

"I told yer. Miserable bastard."

You might think that perhaps Bobby didn't see Jack. I know he did. He looked straight at him. I really wanted them to patch things up that night. I've often thought back to it. What if Sir Bobby had smiled and waved? We might have been able to meet up with him later, but it was not to be.

Jack's strained relationship with his brother is a sad story. They saw each other again when their mother Cissie died in 1996. For many years, Jack had felt that his younger brother didn't do enough for Cissie. There were also issues between Jack and Bobby's wife, Lady Norma.

I can only comment on one side of the story. What I'm sharing with you came from Jack himself. There are certain things that Jack shared with me that I'll never divulge. My respect for him is too great.

I wasn't the only one in Göteborg who had affection for Big Jack. Everyone did!

We were in a bar one night ahead of the Germany versus Holland game the following day. The bar was heaving and when we walked in, they all recognised Big Jack. There were no Germans or Dutch there. They were all Swedes.

A table was cleared for us to sit down and we didn't have to buy so much as a pint. The queue for Jack's autograph stretched to the street outside. It was incredible. A huge guy, who we christened Igor, acted as our minder. Not that we needed protection, it was all good-natured fun.

Then Jack dropped a bombshell.

"I want to go to one of those beer tents."

I was reluctant.

"Not a good idea Jack. There are hundreds of German and Dutch fans in there and they hate each other."

Jack was adamant.

"Come on, we're going. Igor after you."

So we went.

It was a huge marquee jammed full of rival fans with a bar selling Carlsberg along one side. The two "mobs" were facing off, plastic glasses in hand and beer overflowing.

Sarcasm got the better of me.

"Good idea Jack."

We didn't get the chance to leave. The next minute we heard "Itch Jackee Sharlton!"

They all turned to look, and then parted.

It reminded me of that episode of Only Fools and Horses where Del Boy pulled up outside Nelson Mandela House and there was a riot going on. Del blows his horn and the rioters part like the Red Sea to allow him through.

But instead of "It's Del Boy!" all we heard was "Itch Jackee Sharlton!"

Pints came over, in a civilised way. All the aggro just disappeared.

Jack the peacemaker.

"I'm with him, I'm with him" I repeated.

"Show am I!" added Igor.

It was great. They nearly all spoke English too. We were there for about 20 minutes and as we strolled out of the beer tent, all the signs were that hostilities were about to resume. We headed back to our friendly bar in the town centre.

Outside we bumped into Ian St. John and his mate, who was the Pastor of Motherwell Football Club.

After Saint did the introductions, Jack was intrigued by the pastor's credentials. Jack had met Pope John Paul II during Italia 90, when the whole squad visited The Vatican.

"Is that right? Are ya a priest? 'ow high up are ya? 'Cos I know the PURP."

I wouldn't say a typical day in the life of Big Jack, but certainly one I'll never forget.

Nor will Igor.

One person who wasn't feeling a lot of love during Euro 92 was Graham Taylor.

As I knew him well, I felt bad for Graham when the criticism got out of hand. He was such a good man but the media destroyed him. England weren't playing well during this tournament. His tactics and team selection were being questioned.

I was able to interview Graham live on air. He was joined by captain Gary Lineker from their hotel. I was in a studio in Stockholm. England's first match was coming up. The people back home wanted to know if Graham was going to use three at the back, so I asked him.

Graham really took the hump with me.

"That's got nothing to do with you!"

"With respect Graham, I'm asking on behalf of millions of people back home."

You should've seen the look on Lineker's face. It was totally out of character for Graham. But being the boss of England comes with incredible expectations. That had been accentuated by Bobby Robson getting to the World Cup semi-final just two years earlier in Italy.

Snapping at me wasn't a good look for Graham Taylor. Many years later, I was told by Jeff Farmer that Graham not only felt bad about the interview, but he thought that was the beginning of the end for him.

England didn't get out of their group and neither did Scotland. An early exit for both nations. The headline from the loss against Sweden was Lineker being taken off in his last appearance for his country. Alan Smith came on for the captain but couldn't find the goal that would've ensured progress to the semi-finals.

The remarkable tale of the whole tournament was Denmark. They beat the Dutch on penalties to reach the final, facing Germany. The match didn't go as expected. The Danes had shocked everyone by getting that far. They had one more surprise up their sleeve.

Midfielder John Jensen scored one of the goals. Just as Ron Atkinson was criticising him on air for his lack of shooting skills! The 2-0 win was a real shock. At one stage it boiled down to Peter Schmeichel versus Jürgen Klinsmann. The Danes had done it, against all the odds. What a fantastic achievement!

After the match, the Danish fans were in fine voice. Jack and I were live on air and Ron had joined us.

I burst into song along with the Danes:

"Always Look on the Bright Side of Life!!"

Then Jack and Ron started. The three of us finished the coverage for Euro 92 by singing "Always Look on the Bright Side of Life" on national TV.

If they were alive today, both Brian Clough and Tony Bennett would testify that I'm not a great singer.

31

Back home

I loved being over in Sweden, but I needed a rest. I was relaxing in the garden, nursing my bruised face. Then the phone rang. It was The Doc. It was official. ITV no longer had the rights for live top flight football.

The newly branded Premier League was going to be on Sky TV, with Match of the Day showing highlights on Saturday nights. ITV didn't get anything from the new contract. There would still be European club football on ITV and also some England games, but the amount of coverage would be a lot less.

It was a wrench to lose the contract, covering the best of English football. But it was some consolation that Richard Keys got the presenting job for Sky. He's a mate and another Radio City graduate. Keysie's a terrific professional who truly understands the game. His partnership with Andy Gray has got to be the most inciteful on TV.

As the lads are now based in Qatar, we don't get the chance to see them in action every week. All because of some banter that made the public domain when it shouldn't have done. I'm sure they were set up. It was locker room humour. I don't believe they meant any harm. Others have done far worse and kept their job. Donald Trump ended up as the President of the United States of America twice.

My son Chris is studio director for Richard and Andy's show in Doha. Back in the 1980s, Keysie and Clive Tyldesley helped me erect a swing in our back garden for our Chris and Laura.

Strange how things work out!

Now back to 1992.

With ITV the big losers over the TV rights, what would the future hold for me?

No more Sundays doing The Match for a start.

Doc to the rescue.

"It's time for you to come home."

He wanted me to work exclusively for Granada. Don't forget I'd been doing Kick Off after it returned in 1989 and Soccer Night too. To be honest, I'd never really left.

You might think that being back at Granada was a cushy little number and I'd just go through the motions. I couldn't do that. Tony Wilson once said something to me that I'll never forget.

"You're like me. We're red light junkies."

Both Tony and I were addicted to the buzz of being live. When the red light on top of the camera came on, it was an adrenaline rush. I still got nervous before going live. It was like the pre-match jitters that a footballer gets. The excitement of it all. I knew if I ever lost that feeling, it was time to do something else.

Granada produced the quiz show Busman's Holiday, and for the latest series they wanted a new presenter. Sarah Kennedy had done it for a couple of years, replacing original host Julian Pettifer. Apparently, a lot of names were mentioned. The Doc told me to audition for it.

The show had been going since 1985 and had decent ratings. I loved the idea of doing something away from sport. Busman's Holiday was to go out on Mondays at 7 pm, just before the jewel in ITV's crown; Coronation Street.

I'd done recorded TV many times although I preferred the thrill of live television. This was something else. It was gruelling. We recorded thirteen episodes and we did them one after another all in the space of a week.

The shortlist of potential hosts included Bruce Forsyth.

I was told:

"We didn't actually ask Bruce. We thought it would be better to have someone who wouldn't overshadow the contestants. We want them to be the stars of the show, not the host."

I did the audition in the same way as I did the sport. I was laid back. I didn't know any other way. But they wanted more oomph. I began to wonder why they chose me in the first place. I also had to use autocue, which wasn't normal for me.

Those thirteen episodes turned out to be the final series of Busman's Holiday. It was popular and different to other game shows. Basically, it was too expensive for Granada. The company, along with other ITV regions, embarked on cost-cutting measures. The prizes alone, which were working holidays abroad, put the light entertainment department well over budget.

Doing the show did introduce me to a new audience. So to coincide with Busman's Holiday, I appeared as a guest panellist on another ITV programme; "Cluedo". Based around the popular board game, it was presented by Richard Madeley. I knew Richard and Judy fairly well from stints together on Granada Reports.

Two teams, made up of one bloke and one woman, would have to solve the crime. We had to watch a sketch and try and work out who the murderer was, what weapon they used and where they did it. Just like the game.

Against me was the late Steve Wright and Nerys Hughes of "The Liver Birds".

Who did they partner me with? Bella Emberg!

I don't want to be mean but Bella wasn't what you might call a "looker". In fact, she played "Blunderwoman" in Russ Abbot's Madhouse. It was an apt description. But Bella was a lot of fun.

The regulars, who played the characters in the sketch, included Leslie Grantham (Dirty Den from Eastenders), Nicholas Parsons, Jerry Hall and Joanna Lumley.

Anyway, we won and then spent a couple of very enjoyable hours in the green room. At the same time, in a different studio, You've Been Framed was being recorded. Jeremy Beadle made a point of coming into our hospitality room, introduced himself and told me how much he enjoyed Busman's.

Then Jeremy invited me to bring the kids for the following day's recording of You've Been Framed, which we did. After Beadle left, I spent most of the time talking football with Leslie Grantham. You'd never guess he'd served ten years of a life sentence for murder. He came over as such a nice guy.

Richard joined us briefly, but talking football wasn't for him. He didn't hang around when he knew what we were discussing. To give you an idea, on a celebrity edition of Who Wants to Be a Millionaire, the host Jeremy Clarkson asked Richard if there were any subjects he didn't want to crop up.

"Sport."

I found that strange. The Doc initially brought Richard to Granada to present a Rugby League show!

The following year, Richard had his run in with the law when he was arrested for shoplifting. He was all over the newspapers and people still go on about it today. The charge was ridiculous, totally unfounded, and he was acquitted.

It didn't stop his Granada colleagues coming up with a new nickname for the husband-and-wife duo.

Pinch and Judy!

1993 was proving to be a hectic year. The Chief had another idea up his sleeve. "Go For Goal" was a football quiz, just for Granada. The teams of three contestants represented different clubs in the region. It was more of my kind of thing.

I was being kept busy by Granada. I was all over their sports coverage, including Granada Goals Extra, The Granada Match, Soccer Night and of course the bowls. I'd still appear on the evening news, just as I had back in the late 1970s when Tony Wilson gave me my baptism of fire. I loved all of it. I was truly back home.

Being at Granada also introduced me to the wacky world of wrestling. My first experience came in 1979 and I still think I'm paying for it today.

British wrestling was popular at the time. Shown on ITV during World of Sport, grapplers like Big Daddy and Giant Haystacks were household names. We invited the man known as "Mr TV", Jackie Pallo, into the studio. Pallo was famous for his rivalry with Mick McManus.

A ring was set up. The idea being every time he pinned me to the canvas I'd turn to the camera and deliver a line about a sporting event taking place in the North West over the coming weekend. We jostled for a bit of fun. Then he picked me up and did a body slam – the canvas was shaking.

It knocked the stuffing out of me and I'm convinced that was the start of my back issues which still exist to this day. Anyone who suffers with a bad back will know I'm not exaggerating. Back pain is like a dull toothache. You've just got to stop what you're doing, rest and take some painkillers.

So in March 1993, when American wrestling company WCW arrived in Manchester as part of their British tour, I was apprehensive when one of their stars joined us.

It didn't get physical but I nearly had a heart attack!

Johhny B. Badd was our guest. He looked like Little Richard, and he certainly played up to it. Johnny carried with him a device called the "Badd Blaster". About one metre long, it was a glorified party popper. Except I didn't know that.

From out of nowhere, he set it off. It let off such a loud bang that I nearly shit myself! Confetti came flying out of the end of it and went everywhere. It made such a mess that there were still bits of it around the studio for years!

32

Holes not goals

When my career on television took off, my workload increased. There were times when I was doing four or five programmes per week. Factor in the travelling on top of that. I needed to find a way to switch off.

I'd already been playing for a while, but golf became my main form of relaxation. I had a busy schedule, but I made sure that I only played when the kids were at school. The only problem was that it was taking its toll on my back. I'd never suffered before 1979, when Jackie Pallo slammed me. It can't be a coincidence.

Playing golf led me to some unforgettable experiences. As I was a name of sorts, it also meant invites to celebrity/am tournaments, which were always good fun.

One such tournament I played at was in Caldy, near home. It was part of the Ladies European Tour, which was in its infancy. The idea was that there'd be two well-known characters partnering with two lady professionals. It was serious for them, so we amateurs joined in to make a group of four in the first round. I suppose the idea was to get the tournament some publicity for the remaining three rounds.

I was drawn with Andy King to join up with Mickey Walker and another professional, who I can't remember. Ms Walker was a founding member of the tour and went on to captain four Solheim Cup teams. Andy was just about aware that you hit the ball with a stick!

Ms Walker was deadly serious. On one of the early greens, she was lining up a putt.

"Will you move to the side."

"Sure."

"The other way."

"Okay."

"Not there."

I shrugged my shoulders.

"Further."

"I tell you what, why don't I stand in the fuckin' bunker!??"

Kingy was beside himself and barely another word was spoken until we got to the clubhouse. And that was just between me and Kingy. The 19th hole was a blessing.

Another tournament was at Royal Liverpool Golf Course in Hoylake. It's fantastic and is now back on the rota for our Open Championship. This time it was two celebrities teaming up with two money-laden businessmen who paid for the privilege. The money went to charity.

My "celebrity" partner was Frank Carson. In the group behind was Jimmy Hill. Jimmy and I had identical bags. Our names were on the side. I'd say that at least a dozen times, and I'm not exaggerating, when I went to my bag on the following hole, Jimmy's putter was in there.

"Your putter, Jimmy."

"Oh Christ, have I done it again?"

Nice man if a bit forgetful.

Meanwhile Frank was on a roll. Gag after gag for over four hours.

"There was this Irish fellah..."

Non-stop.

We eventually got to the clubhouse and the four of us sat down for some liquid refreshment before dinner and the prize-giving.

Cue Frank:

"Have you heard the one...?"

He was in full flow again. Not only that but we'd heard most of the jokes out on the course already. Then came dinner. Brookside actor Vince Earl was the compere.

He introduced our special guest.

Frank Carson!

No!! I couldn't stand it any longer. Frank was never ending.

"In fact, cracker, a cracker, nicky nacky, Frank Carson...News at Ten...Hoylake."

I didn't win much as a golfer, probably because my six handicap should've been ten. I certainly wasn't a bandit. My proudest moment was winning Heswall Golf Club's Two Generations Cup with my son, Chris. It was foursomes, alternate shots, and we shot a gross 74.

Any golfer will tell you that's a hell of a score in that format of the game. Two over par was a club record for that particular tournament at the time. Foursomes are difficult. Chris is a good golfer, he's in low single figures, and plays with Andy Gray in Qatar.

Someone else who enjoyed a round was Kenny Dalglish. For as long as I can remember, Kenny has called me "Stilts". For years I didn't know why. Until one day, I asked him.

You can also wait for the answer.

Kenny's public persona is nothing like the real deal. He could be a nightmare to interview, because you could barely work out what he was saying, such was his tight-lipped Glaswegian accent.

After one game at Anfield, I caught up with him for an interview while he was carrying his young son, Paul, who'd be about two at the time.

At one point Paul mumbled something and made a grab for the mic.

I looked at Kenny and said: "I understand him better than you."

Kenny loved it. He enjoyed the way he was perceived. He thought it was funny. But when he wanted to, he could express himself most eloquently.

That reminds me of one horrible moment in 1991. I was on the golf course at Heswall when Joyce came running across two fairways and the practise ground.

She was out of breath.

"It's...Kenny Dalglish...he's.... (panting)."

What I thought she said was:

"It's...Kenny Dalglish...he's...died."

I dropped everything and legged it to the pro's shop.

"Alright Elt? Have you heard? Kenny Dalglish's resigned."

"Fucking hell! Is that it?"

I was so relieved.

After Bruce Grobbelaar's testimonial golf day at Heswall, Kenny asked if Joyce and I would give him and his wife Marina a guided tour of the area. He wanted to look at properties.

The theme tune to Neighbours started playing in my mind.

He was just curious. Kenny has always been happy in Southport. We ended up at a village on the Wirral called Thornton Hough, for the night's celebratory dinner. We were chatting and he said how much he'd enjoyed the course and fancied giving it another go. On the day, I'd asked a mate of mine, Geoff Cook, to make up a four-ball. We didn't know who Kenny was bringing.

When he arrived, he introduced us to his partner for the day. The West Lancashire Amateur Match Play Champion!

You see, Kenny didn't like losing.

In fact, he and his mate won 7&6, which is pretty comfortable. With the match over, and with £20 winnings in his pocket, we continued to play the full eighteen holes. On one green, he asked me to read a putt. Now at Heswall, if in doubt the putts tend to go towards the river Dee. That's the line Kenny decided to take.

I decided to give him some advice.

"Not this one Ken, it goes the other way."

I was lying.

Bugger me, he did what I told him and holed the putt. He's just a natural winner. I'll say this however, off a handicap of thirteen, he's a bandit!

So why has he always called me Stilts?

"I was once talking to Elton John and he was wearing these platform boots. It's like he was on stilts. Chatting to him I thought of you, Stilts."

Is that it? Bloody Hell!

In the middle of the 1990s, with optimism back after the FA Cup win over Manchester United, Everton held a golf day, with all proceeds going to various charities. I was in the same four-ball as Duncan Ferguson. He wasn't a golfer but entered into the spirit of the day as you'd expect. He could hit the ball okay, in fact when he really connected, it went a long way.

When we arrived at the "long drive hole" Duncan took out his four iron.

"Dunc there's a prize on this hole for the longest drive, use your driver."

"Nah I'm happy with the four iron, wee man."

He always called me wee man.

Whack!

I'm not sure how far it actually went, it was over 200 yards but most importantly it ended up on the fairway. Anywhere in the rough or semi rough didn't count. There were a few of those, so Big Dunc hit the longest drive with a four iron!

He reminded me of Happy Gilmore.

After the golf, we all had a few drinks before dinner, the entertainment and an auction. There were various bits of memorabilia being auctioned off.

Now when the first one went going, going gone for £150, Dunc put his hand up.

"I'll double it."

Sold to Duncan Ferguson!

About ten items sold in total, and Duncan did the same for each and every one.

Not all went for £150, of course. A normal winning bid would be about £100. So that cost Dunc £200. He contributed a good few grand to the charities that night.

He didn't want any credit though.

"Don't make a fuss about it, wee man. If it helps, "m just happy to do it."

He's idolised by Evertonians, and to this day if he's asked to send a video message to someone less fortunate, he always obliges.

Duncan Ferguson. A Blue to the core.

Then there was someone who epitomised the red side of Merseyside.

Gerry Marsden.

For those of you that don't know, Gerry was the singer of the group Gerry and the Pacemakers, who followed in the footsteps of The Beatles in the Swinging Sixties, which was also known as the Merseybeat era.

Their most famous song? You'll Never Walk Alone.

Gerry lived close by and we often crossed paths. He enjoyed his golf and on one occasion we played together in an event for the British Heart Foundation. We were first out as Gerry had a gig in Scotland later that night. It was terribly cold.

On the sixth tee he took a flask out of his bag.

"Here you go Elt, this'll warm you up."

It was rocket fuel. The rest of the round was a bit of a blur.

Gerry told me his plan was to sleep on the way to the home of Scotch whisky, probably to replenish the "brew" we'd consumed that morning at Heswall Golf Course. We'd arranged to meet up the following week for a spot of clay pigeon shooting on the outskirts of Chester. He brought his wife's gun for me. Both Gerry and Pauline were regular visitors to the shooting range.

"Go 'ead... I'll trigger the bird, you shoot it."

So I did what I was told.

Bullseye!

"Fuck off! You've done this before! Terrific shot."

It was a fluke, which I proved time and time again as the little clay pigeons sailed through the air and landed totally unscathed!

Of course, Gerry will always be remembered for "You'll Never Walk Alone". At Ronnie Moran's testimonial, I was on the pitch at Anfield alongside Gerry as he belted it out.

Or so I thought.

"Sounding good there, Gerry."

"I'm miming yer soft twat!"

God bless you Gerry!

Mark Hughes was someone I got to know better as his career as a player wound down. Then he stepped into management. When he was the boss at Manchester City, we played golf together at Mere Golf and Country Club. It was a huge charity event.

Some backroom guy at City found Mark by one of the greens and told him they'd signed Robinho.

As quick as a flash, Mark replied:

"I don't fuckin' want him."

City had just been taken over by Sheik Monsour and I couldn't help thinking to myself his days were numbered. New managers normally follow new owners.

Look at Birmingham. John Eustace was doing a fabulous job. In comes the consortium involving the legendary NFL quarterback, Tom Brady. Eustace gets toe ended out of St. Andrews. In comes Wayne Rooney and they get relegated.

As I feared, Mark Hughes left City the following year.
I managed to play golf for a few more years, until my back made it impossible.

33

On the road again

After all the travelling I'd done while working for ITV, you'd think that I'd be happy to stay closer to home. But when opportunities came up to take part in after-dinner speaking events with some of the legends of the game, I didn't think twice.

I first started getting asked to do gentleman's evenings in the 1980s. With the results service and then The Match, I became a recognisable name to book. This also helped me to reconnect with some old friends. One of them was Liverpool's Tommy Smith. We'd remained friends from back in the days of me travelling with the club in the 1970s.

Bill Shankly knew how tough Tommy was.

"Tommy Smith wasn't born. He was quarried."

Tommy was part of one of the most surreal experiences of my career. I was prominent on Granada's programming, and a decision was made to do "Elton Welsby Day".

It was flattering.

There was an Antique's Roadshow style event with Mark Owen. Held at Albert Dock in Liverpool, people brought football memorabilia and had it valued. We saw some weird and wonderful things that day.

The highlight was a sportsman's evening, held at the same place. I was the presenter. It was a full black tie do. We did it as if everyone had already eaten. But there was no meal. There was just wine, cheese and biscuits on the table. It looked terrific and authentic.

Tommy and Duncan McKenzie were the two former players invited to speak. They didn't hold back.

For example:

Tommy confronted a referee.

"What if I called you a twat?"

"I'd send you off!"

"What if I think you're a twat?"

"I couldn't do anything."

"I think you're a twat!"

Years later, in 2007, and to coincide with the 30th anniversary of Liverpool's first European Cup win, Tommy organised events for some of the Liverpool Supporters' Clubs. He asked me to host.

There were also his ex-teammates Jimmy Case, Joey Jones and Ian Callaghan. I'd been friends with all of them since Radio City. We travelled up and down the country, doing the same routine.

I always kicked off the show, then Tommy would interrupt me:

"Wait a minute Elt, what are you doing here? You're an Everton fan!"

"Hold on Tommy! I commentated on every one of those European games, including the final. I've got every right to be here!"

A pleasant surprise from these evenings was how funny Joey Jones was. He had no problem doing public speaking. Joey was a natural. He referred to the famous banner from the final in Rome. It's even called the Scouse Bayeux tapestry!

"Joey Ate the Frogs Legs Made the Swiss Roll Now He's Munching Gladbach."

As far as I know, Joey still has it at his home.

My experiences with Tommy weren't just to do with Liverpool. He joined Jack Charlton and myself when we went to the Isle of Man for another evening. It was billed as "Football's Hard Men". We were having a drink after this particular show at an Irish pub in Douglas, when Big Jack started telling us a story about Sven-Göran Eriksson. He'd never shared this with us before. He'd not used it in any of his shows either.

When Sven got the England job, Jack was asked what he thought about a foreigner being appointed. Jack simply said that he thought it should've been an Englishman. Not long afterwards, the two bumped into each other. Jack saw this as his chance to put his side of the story over to Sven. He introduced himself thinking it was the first time they'd met.

"Jackie, don't you recognise me? I came to observe your training methods when you were at Sheffield Wednesday. I stayed at your house."

Big Jack had forgotten all about it.

When he told us, Tommy and I burst out laughing. We knew Jack wasn't great with names, but Sven had even stayed with him! We both told Jack to put it into his next show. He used it every time after that.

While writing this book, sadly Sven-Göran Eriksson lost his fight against cancer and passed away in August 2024. The way he handled his illness showed him to be a man of great strength and dignity.

Jack Charlton was one of the most popular people when it came to after dinner speaking gigs. He was also one of the best. When Bob Carter was captain at Heswall golf club he pulled me to one side and asked me for help. He wanted to make his captain's dinner a big extravaganza.

"Who can you get to be the principal speaker? I want a sports star, preferably a footballer."

"Leave it with me, Mr Captain."

I rang Jack. He was the obvious choice.

"Sorry, son. I'm booked to speak at a function in Westminster. I can't let the Prime Minister down. Try Banksy. He's a good 'un."

So I got in touch with Gordon Banks. He agreed to do it. There was one condition; he wanted to play the course in the afternoon. Now that was pretty easy to arrange, as we'd be playing with the captain.

The day arrived. It was pissing it down. I met Banksy and told him that with the weather against us, I'd reserved the snooker room. Not a chance! Gordon wanted to play golf, despite the most inclement weather imaginable.

It was cold, wet and windy. We set off with the captain, his mate, Gordon and myself. Nobody else. There wasn't another soul stupid enough to play. We got round in just under three hours, drenched and freezing. We changed and hit the bar for a few hot toddies.

Bloody hell, they were needed!

Then it was a taxi back to mine, where Banksy and I had another couple of drinks. We got suited and booted, before returning to the clubhouse for 7:30 pm.

Gordon was super. He shook hands with just about everyone before we all sat down. I'd got the taste, so I carried on drinking. By the time it came for me to introduce the captain's guest of honour, I was slurring a bit. I made reference to the "fucking weather". I got ticked off for swearing. It was okay for our guest speaker, but not for one of the members.

It seems that every time I did the club a favour I'd be in the wrong.

Banksy took to his feet at about 9:30 pm and sat down to thunderous applause. About 45 minutes later, I was certainly back in the captain's good books.

Gordon told the story of his out-of-this-world save from Pelé in the 1970 World Cup.

Jairzinho down the right, a pinpoint cross, Pelé leaping and heading it downward into the corner.

Surely a goal!

No!

Gordon scrambling back to the far post. Letting the ball bounce. Then scooping it over the bar.

It's become renowned as the greatest save of all time.

The punchline came from Banksy:

"You know what, gentlemen? Alan Mullery looked down at me as I was getting to my feet and said:

'Fucking hell Banksy! Why didn't you hold it?'"

Jack might not have been free on that occasion. But his time at Heswall Golf Club would come.

Being a Blue didn't prevent me from being asked to take part in Ronnie Moran's testimonial. Part of the celebrations took us to the Europa Hotel in Belfast. Stan Boardman came with us, as did former Gladiator Mike Ahearne, who was known as Warrior on the show. The hotel was packed.

Stan did his routine. And began telling jokes about religion. My heart sank. I started looking for the exits at the most bombed hotel in Europe.

I needn't have worried. The audience loved it. They were able to laugh at each other. Nobody got angry or took offence. Stan was helping the peace process more than anyone had before!

The following morning, Warrior and I went to play golf. We were scheduled to leave Belfast around 4 pm. Getting back to the hotel in plenty of time, we couldn't find Stan. I checked with the concierge.

"Any idea where Stan Boardman is?"

"Oh yes sir, he went out about forty-five minutes ago. That pub over there."

There was no sign of him in the pub, so I searched out the landlord.

"Excuse me, have you seen Stan Boardman by any chance?"

"He's been in oiright. He did about five minutes telling jokes and moved on."

After entertaining the punters in this place, he'd gone on to another one. We arrived at the next boozer. The conversation with the landlord was the same. Stan had been. More gags. And he'd gone.

This continued until the fourth pub. We finally found him in there!

Stan and I have worked together many times.

We were driven to Wigan RLFC for a leaving do for their legendary coach, John Monie. There was a huge marquee erected over the Central Park pitch. As I was walking round to the entrance a little old member of the ground staff was forking the perimeter.

"He were in touch, tha' knows."

"What? Who?"

"Van Vollenhoven, he were in touch."

I believe he was referring to the 1961 Challenge Cup Final at Wembley where Tom Van Vollenhoven of St. Helens scored a sensational try to help inflict defeat on Wigan. The old chap obviously knew I was a Saints supporter.

But do me a favour, that was 1961. He was telling me this 32 years later!

I suppose that underlines the intense rivalry between St. Helens and Wigan.

As for the function itself, it was a marathon. It seemed everyone connected with Monie and Wigan took to the mic to pay tribute. I did my bit, but Stan was there to close down proceedings with thirty-five minutes of comedy.

He didn't get on until about one-thirty in the morning. By which time, our driver was pissed. So about half past two, after finding someone who wasn't hammered, we were driven around Wigan looking for a motel.

It was a long night!

34

Balls up

I've had one or two moments in front of the camera that I don't look back on too fondly. One of those came very early on in my career.

I've talked so much about The Doc's hits. He had plenty of them. Then there was "Good Evening Elton". After doing well on the two Kick Off shows, The Doc decided that I should do a chat show, Parkinson style.

The idea sounded fine in principle. It turned out to be terrible.

The Doc chose Freddie Pye as his first guest.

For those who don't know who he was, Freddie had been chairman at Stockport County and Wigan Athletic. A local scrap merchant, who loved football, Freddie would later become vice chairman at Manchester City.

It was the wrong choice.

Freddie was very nervous and it showed. He wasn't the only one. There were about sixty people in the audience watching us almost freeze. I stuck with the questions that I'd written down in advance. I didn't listen to Freddie's answers nor adapt my line of questioning.

What a mess!

The second guest had more name value; boxer John Conteh. A former world champion and very charismatic. We gave John a big introduction, including a two-minute video package. Edited by Neil Bowker, it showed Conteh's background and rise to fame. I wasn't prepared for what happened next.

John Conteh burst into tears.

He refused to continue the interview. I hadn't even said one word yet!

The Doc talked to him for about ten minutes to try and get him to do it. He finally accepted as long as the studio audience was removed. He then proceeded to rant at boxing's "merchants" who were ruining his career.

Then he left.

"Good Evening Elton" bit the dust.

In the 1990s, after Doc had retired and McDowell had inflicted so much damage on the sports department, Jeff Anderson breathed new life into it.

"Talking Balls" was born. A chat show with a panel of guests and a live studio audience. It was terrific. It's without doubt one of the most satisfying things I've ever done.

Don't forget this was a regional show, but we still managed to pull off the coup of having legendary boxer "Marvelous" Marvin Hagler on. Okay, he wasn't in the studio, he joined us by satellite, but what a guest!

He'd legally changed his name to Marvelous Marvin Hagler and I'd totally forgotten. During the discussion, we all called him Marvin. There was one exception. Another guest was ex-Everton player Adrian Heath. "Inchy" addressed Hagler as Marvelous. Creep!

I have to give a lot of credit to Ged Clarke, who booked people to come on Talking Balls. He did an excellent job. One of the guests was Geoffrey Boycott. An icon of cricket and the county of Yorkshire, Boycott was booked to appear at the same time as Lancashire and Pakistan bowler Wasim Akram. Boycott made a comment to Wasim that I won't repeat.

Politically incorrect is an understatement.

I think Geoffrey, being of a certain age, thought it was funny and acceptable.

It wasn't.

Thankfully, there were plenty of highs.

Having Peter Reid and Ian Botham on together was a lot of fun. The two of them got on like a house on fire. We showed an old clip from 1978 of Reidy from his Bolton days. After getting promoted, The Doc was interviewing the players in the dressing room. Bolton had narrowly missed out the year before to Brian Clough's Forest.

Paul was going around the team. He went over to Peter Reid.

"What a difference a year makes Peter."

"Oh yeah, that's a great song."

Then he started to sing it.

"What a difference a day makes,
twenty-four little hours."

After the clip finished, we went straight to a close up of Reidy. He was shaking his head and cringing, but he saw the funny side.

And I hadn't finished yet.

"Do you remember when you dyed your hair to cover up going grey?"

"What's all this? Are you ganging up on me? So I look like Roy Orbison, so what?"

That's what Talking Balls was like.

By now, you know that golf was a huge part of my life for a long time. So with that in mind, I did another Granada exclusive based around the sport. It was another short-lived project. But it was brilliant to be part of.

Known as "It's Your Round", the programme revolved around well-known sports personalities chatting to me while playing. Naturally the guests had a connection to the North West.

It was filmed at Heswall Golf Club. Where else?

I'd already done something similar as a one-off in my early days on Kick Off. And I had to pinch myself when I did.

I went round with Harry Catterick, Howard Kendall and Alan Ball that day. That's something I'll never forget. It was only a short TV segment, but it lasted a lot longer in reality. These men were heroes of mine. It was fascinating too. Both Bally and Howard were picking Harry's brains about management. I would chip in from time to time, just to keep things flowing along.

When "It's Your Round" was launched, we had Big Jack, Steve Bruce, Alex Murphy, Francis Lee, Kevin Keegan and John Parrot.

Big Jack was first up. He could've stayed at mine, but my spare bed wasn't big enough!

Hearing that Jack was going to be here overnight, Len Ellison, who was the chairman of social activities at the club, came to me with an interesting proposal.

"Do you think that Jack would do an evening here? You know, before you record the next day?"

I pointed out that Jack's fee for a speech night was £2,000.

"I can't afford that! Can you see what you can do?"

It was all sorted and for £400.

"I'm there anyway, so I'll do it."

We had a great meal and everyone was enjoying themselves. Now it was time for me to introduce Jack. And he played all his greatest hits. The members loved it.

He talked about the best player he ever saw. His own brother Bobby.

"You remember that wonderful goal he scored against Mexico in the World Cup? The one where he ran from inside his own half. Then he went and put it in. Twenty-five yards he was. Right in the top corner. The place went mad. What people don't remember is, I gave him the ball."

When the event finished, and before I got him back to where he was staying, Jack and I had one for the road. Len Ellison came over to thank him.

"Jack, that was fantastic. That's the best night we've ever had here."

Len pulled an envelope out of his pocket with Jack's money and gave it to him.

"Do you know? I enjoyed it so much, I'd have done it for nothing."

Len grabbed me by my arm.

"He said he'd have done it for nothing!! You've just cost this club £400!!"

My reply to Len did not show the kind of etiquette and manners associated with a golf club!

There were some things that Jack told me that he didn't use in his act. One of them included his infamous black book.

The book didn't actually exist.

Jack did confess privately that he had certain people in mind that he wanted for revenge. But he never wrote anything down. The one name he gave me was Everton's Johnny Morrissey. "Mogsy" was top of the list.

Jack was even charged by the FA for bringing the game into disrepute about "the black book".

He got off and rightly so.

I was doing a charity event at West Derby golf club for Zoe's Place, a hospice for terminally ill kids. I didn't know in advance that Lady Derby was going to be there. My routine was known for being "adult". The F word was used a lot. I spoke to her beforehand and explained. She laughed and told me to just do what I normally would do.

Perfect. The green light from Lady Derby.

"Good evening gentleman. I have some bad news to start with, I'm afraid.

You know, with Lady Derby being here, the golf club secretary has advised me not to use any bad language.

If I do, he reckons he'll get the sack.

So what I want to do now gentleman, is organise a whip round for his fucking leaving present!"

We finished with an auction. A good amount was raised for the charity. And Lady Derby had the last laugh.

"I'll pay £200 to the cause, if Elton Welsby gets his hair dyed red."

I went to Zoe's Place and did exactly that.

I was playing golf the following day. I arrived at the course and the club's main benefactor was there, a man named Stuart Cookson. He was terribly posh. He also wanted everyone to follow the rules of the club, to the strictest degree.

We were at the first tee and he was looking at me strangely. I didn't understand why. I'd completely forgotten about my red hair.

"Is there a problem Stuart?"

"I've noticed your HAIR. What is all THAT about?"

So I told him the story.

"Good for YOU old chap."

And we teed off as normal.

35

Full circle

Things were changing at Granada TV. The Doc had been gone for a while and of course Paul McDowell too.

One of the best things I did at Granada in the 1990s was the Granada Goals Extra show. As it went out not long after the final whistles had blown, there were a fair few on-air mistakes. I thought that the ITV Results Service was chaotic at times.

This was far crazier.

It started it in 1991. Bob Greaves presented the very first one. Rob McCaffrey, Jim Beglin and Clive Tyldesley also worked on it, doing commentaries, reports and voiceovers.

At the same time as that first show, I was doing bowls at Ellesmere Port with Jean Doherty. It was only about twenty minutes from home. When we arrived at my place, The Doc and Clive Tyldesley were already there.

Paul passed me the tape.

"Look at this."

It was so bad it was hilarious. Jean and I were laughing our heads off. Paul looked like he wanted to kill us both! Bob was out of his comfort zone. It was nothing like Granada Reports. No autocue, no running order, whichever goals package was ready came next. He was all over the place. It was a car crash. The Doc should've realised the show needed a specialist. When I took over, I thoroughly enjoyed it.

The ultimate challenge.

Sometimes, we'd cut to the wrong match. If we did have the right pictures, the commentary might be at the wrong speed. I remember back referencing one match and crediting Pinky and Perky with the commentary!

Granada Goals Extra ran for seven years.

As the 1990s drew to a close, we had a different show; Soccer Sunday. The best part about it was the guests, we had a different one every week. Including Sir Alex Ferguson. That was a highlight for me.

It's on that programme that I worked with an old favourite for a final time.

Producer Jonathan Parry had formed a friendship with Nigel Clough when Liverpool toured South Africa for a documentary. They'd even met Nelson Mandela as part of it. Jonathan wanted Nigel to come on Soccer Sunday with his dad. I was all for it. But when Nigel asked, Clough senior wasn't certain. Apparently, when Brian was told that it was going to be with me, he said yes. I hope that's true!

Cloughie looked almost a shadow of his former self, but his wit was as sharp as ever. He came out with one or two gems, mainly at Nigel's expense. Nigel didn't mind at all. I got the impression he was glad his dad was well enough to take part. Clough senior lived up to his reputation as being the best interviewee in football.

Once again, I got away unscathed!

Cloughie always kept me on my toes. I never knew what he was going to say or do next. A few years earlier at the City Ground, I was chatting to Brian's assistant Ronnie Fenton near Cloughie's office.

Then I heard a familiar voice.

"Welsby! Shithead!"

"What have I done?" I asked Ronnie.

"Don't worry about that, it means he likes you. Brian's a bit funny like that."

If that was his way of being nice, I'd hate to have been on the receiving end if he bore a grudge! He could cut you in half with his tongue. To this day, I look back on our encounters with enormous affection. That appearance on Soccer Sunday was the last time I ever saw him.

He truly was a one-off.

The ratings for Soccer Sunday weren't great. When that happens, the pressure starts to build.

One segment wasn't to my liking.

Alistair Mann covered Sunday League football. I thought it was a terrible idea and a waste of three minutes. It turned out to be a success. Guests came on the show and thought it was great.

I got that one wrong.

Sue Woodward was head of local programming. We didn't get on very well. She enforced the rules and broke them herself. When it was no-smoking in the office, she still lit up.

She also had a problem with me.

One Monday, Jim Belgin and I were on together, doing Granada Reports. We did a round-up of the football. Beforehand Jim and I had gone through it. Everything was fine.

Woodward was producing the show. I heard her in my earpiece.

"Get Elton to put his links into the computer."

"I don't have any. I just have a few notes written down. It's ad lib."

"Just put it in the fucking computer!!"

It was too late to do it. We were about twenty minutes from going live.

I didn't think anything of it.

The memory came back to me in May 2000 though. Woodward called me in to see her. She explained that Soccer Sunday wasn't doing well. The ratings weren't great apparently.

"When the audience numbers drop, you have to make a choice. Change the show or change the presenter. Now I actually think that the show is quite good."

I knew what was coming.

"We will not be requiring you to do it again next season."

"What are you saying?"

"The show's popular. You're not."

"So for twenty years I've been unpopular?"

"No, errm..."

She didn't have an answer.

"Your time's up."

I wasn't out of options. A group of radio stations had been launched in different areas of the country during the 1990s. One of them was 105.4 Century, which represented the North West. It was still building its audience and reputation. When they decided to cover football, the chance arose for me to go back on the airwaves.

I stayed there for two years. The first year was great. The second one? Not so much.

They even used my name. "Elton Welsby's Soccer Saturday" was born. We also did a show on a Sunday.

I was joined by ex-players. We had Gary Owen, Graeme Sharp, Mickey Thomas and Alan Kennedy. We would discuss the action or the latest news. Fans could phone in to give their thoughts or ask one of the lads a question. It was a lot of fun, factual, informative and even a bit heated at times.

I introduced the idea of doing a quiz. The switchboard lit up with callers wanting to take part. Journalist Alan Nixon and former Manchester United goalkeeper Alex Stepney were involved. It lasted two hours and it flew by.

For the first season of the Saturday show, I did two hours of build-up before the games. There was a new idea for the second season. Marcus Buckland did the first hour, which was aired on all the Century stations around the country. The second hour would return to the regional studios. I had to listen to Buckland before taking over for hour two. It just didn't work. He was more suited to tennis.

When my run at Century ended, I was still doing after-dinner work. But something wasn't right. I missed the buzz. The red-light junkie needed his fix.

Ironically, I returned to Granada. But only as a guest. Actor Ricky Tomlinson was going on a theatre tour doing "An Evening with Jim Royle". I was to be his straight man. So they had both of us on to plug the tour. Matt Smith introduced me as a "legend in these parts". I wondered if the Woodward woman was watching.

The tour with Ricky was certainly different. We'd pick him up from his home in Liverpool. Then he'd sleep in the car until we got to the venue. We'd do two hours. Then he'd get his head down again on the way home.

When he wasn't asleep, Ricky was good company. We'd do an hour and Ricky would be in character dressed as Jim Royle.

It was after the interval when things turned sour.

Ricky went more into his personal life and his past. He talked about his political beliefs and his time in prison. It was autobiographical. But it wasn't Jim Royle. We received a number of complaints. People were asking for refunds. I was told by the promoter Roy Hastings to sort it out.

So after that, when Ricky started to go off on a tangent, I'd guide him back to Jim Royle. I'd ask the audience for their favourite bit of The Royle Family. At every show it was the bit where Jim and Twiggy danced to Mambo No. 5 while decorating.

Cue the music.

Ricky and I would get up and start dancing. The crowd loved it. Even if Ricky's arse was hanging out the back of his jeans.

I don't think Ricky realised that the audience didn't give a shit about his story. When he stuck to Jim Royle, the punters went home happy. We did the rest of the dates without a hitch.

I'd always been keen to work for Everton in some capacity. It made perfect sense. So I became presenter of Everton TV. Sometimes what appears to be a dream job, doesn't work out like that. My time at Everton was disappointing.

I knew the job wasn't for me when we went over to Monaco for a sports fair. After we finished our work, my boss Mark Rowan told me that we'd done for the day. He suggested going for a beer. I asked him again if he was sure there was nothing else to do. He was clear on it.

I asked because I never used to drink before or during a show. Unlike Lord John Oaksey!

Mark booked a table for six at a restaurant, overlooking the marina. We all relaxed and one drink became a few. We were laughing and joking and tucking into a mountain of seafood, which had been recommended by Graeme Sharp. We had some more beer and wine with the meal. We must've stayed there for a good three hours.

We returned to the hotel. I was knackered. Time for bed.

Except that wasn't Mr Rowan's plan. He wanted me to do the voiceovers there and then. I reminded him that he'd said that we'd finished for the day. Now he wanted to get back to work. Nobody was in the right state to do it.

Reluctantly, I agreed. After recording the first two, I asked to listen to them. I was slurring, sounding more like Dean Martin. I got the cameraman to wipe everything. We did it the next day. And it was fine.

During the season I spent with the club, one of the few highlights was meeting and interviewing Sylvester Stallone.

He was promoting Rocky Balboa, the sixth film of the Rocky series. He was with Everton shareholder, Robert Earl. The Planet Hollywood restaurant chain was Earl's brainchild and involved Stallone and a few other Hollywood A-listers.

Sly, as I was asked to call him, walked out onto the pitch brandishing an Everton scarf high above his head.

The crowd responded with chants of "Rocky, Rocky!!"

Or was it "Rambo, Rambo!!"

We arranged a half-time interview. Of course, I got one cheeky question in.

"Sly, as you probably know we have an American goalkeeper (Tim Howard), and he says he was inspired by you."

"Oh right, 'ow da ya work that out?"

"Escape to Victory."

Sly smiled. He just about got it.

Honestly though, there was only thing that I did while at Everton that I'm truly proud of. I produced and presented a tribute to Alan Ball after he died in 2007. Everton were at home to Manchester United. We did about an hour leading up to kick-off. I was determined that the tribute to Bally would be a fitting one. He deserved it.

But wait a minute, you're reading something called Game For A Laugh!

I can assure you that this book isn't going to finish on a downer.

36

The last laugh

My career in journalism lasted over four decades. Not bad when you consider I was a hospital porter with no direction in life.

Paul Doherty was more than a mentor. He was like a guardian angel watching over me. He knew what I could do. I'd never have achieved half of what I did without The Doc. And yet I wasn't immune to his famous bollockings.

Granada Soccer Night was a very popular programme in the North West, with highlights of all the night's games from around the region and presented live. The running time was anywhere between one and two hours, depending on the number of games. On one occasion, we were rapidly approaching midnight. There was one match to go.

"Coming up after the break, a cracking game from Maine Road, so you've got a couple of minutes to make yourselves a hot chocolate. Stay with us."

Through my earpiece I could hear the phone ring in the studio gallery.

Doc answered.

"Hi Malcolm. Say again? Really? I'll tell him NOW!"

With that he hurtled out of the door, and down the stairs to confront me.

"Never go to a fuckin' break like that again!!"

"Pardon?"

I had no idea what he was on about. I'd just ad-libbed and had no clue what I'd actually said.

"You've just told those who are still watching not to watch the adverts and make a cup of hot fuckin' chocolate!

I've just had the head of sales on the phone and he's fuckin' fuming!

Those adverts pay your fuckin' wages.

Don't say anything like that AGAIN!!"

For the record, I never did.

Paul Doherty's legacy is all over film and television. He mentored so many.

I've already mentioned Wayne Garvie. Paul Greengrass is another. He went to Hollywood, directing the Jason Bourne films and projects with Tom Hanks. TV directors such as Richard Signy and Tracey Rooney came through the ranks of the sports department while I was the anchor man.

Jason Ferguson is another who owes a lot to The Doc. His dad does too. Sir Alex struggled with the media in his early days at Old Trafford. He went to Paul for advice. The Chief, despite being a Manchester City fan, guided Fergie through it. He wasn't the only one. Advice was always available to the likes of newsreader Anna Ford, Michael Parkinson and David "Diddy" Hamilton.

I've said it many times. Paul Doherty was the hardest man I've ever known. The Doc didn't flinch. Even if you a were big name. He was the ultimate professional.

Jeremy Guscott was hired to cover some rugby for us. It was quite a coup to get the former England international and pin-up of the sport.

In his analysis, he said "I think..."

The Chief jumped in.

"I'm not paying you to think. I'm paying you to know."

Paul's vision of bringing bowls into our homes was successful. And he wanted more. The Doc decided Super Bowl should be more showbiz. To give life to it, Graham C.

Williams came in to direct it. He was famous within TV for directing Spitting Image.

There was one thing The Doc insisted on though. We don't change the game itself.

One idea was to bring in people from outside of bowls. That included a celebrity competition. It wasn't going to be televised, it was for the crowd only. So the match was booked. Cricket versus darts. Bob Willis and Ian Botham against Eric Bristow and Jocky Wilson. All popular, all well known.

Ian came up and joined me to watch the competitive bowls matches. We weren't on air. He just wanted a good vantage point and mine was undoubtedly the best.

At the same time, Jocky Wilson was in hospitality. And he was enjoying it a little too much. The Doc could see where this was going. He confronted Wilson's agent. Paul made it clear, under no circumstances does Jocky get pissed.

About two hours later, it was time to get the four lads ready for their game of bowls. Someone went to fetch Jocky from hospitality. He was out of it. The Doc was notified and he legged it to see what state Wilson was in.

Paul found Wilson slumped in a chair, totally pissed with fag ash all down his shirt. He was mumbling. And making no sense. There were a lot of people in that room, including Granada hierarchy. The Doc couldn't lay into Wilson in front of everyone.

The agent was there as well. Their discussion continued in the car park. The Doc returned. The agent didn't.

The remaining players had a go at the bowls, and the public were just happy to see the three of them.

Jocky seemed like a nice man but he didn't do himself any favours. He made an appearance on Bullseye once, where he was drinking and smoking.

He was lucky to hit the board.

When you spend a long time in TV, there are always going to be uncomfortable moments. There'll be times when you mess up. And there's nothing you can do about it. When it's live, there's no hiding place.

One example springs to mind.

"And now the goals from Carrow Road, where the game finished 0-0."

I call it a brain fart. I was probably already thinking ahead.

After a Manchester United match, I went to interview Kevin Moran. Kevin was a warrior. He was always going in where it hurts and often came off worse. On this particular occasion, he was bloody and bruised.

I turned to local journalist Eddie Booth.

"Eddie, is Kevin Moran married?"

"Yeah, yeah Elt. He is, yeah."

So I went to speak to Kevin.

"Kevin, what does your wife say when you come home bloodied and bruised after nearly every game?"

"Not much Elton, I'm not married."

Yeah, thanks Eddie!

When Doc asked me about my cock-up, he wanted to know where I got the info from. When I told him, he shook his head:

"Fuckin' hell! You can't rely on Eddie!"

Years later, a trip to Old Trafford led to me coming very close to the infamous Fergie hairdryer.

I'd done the voiceover on United's previous match, a 3-1 away victory. I said something along the lines of the score flattered United. A one goal cushion would've been more fitting and reflected better on their opponents. That's all.

At the next home match, I was with The Doc and went into Fergie's office, as was normal. As soon as we arrived, Fergie fixed his eyes on me. I could see he wasn't in the best of moods.

"Hey! What's this aboot ye saying we didnae deserve to win last week!?!!"

I was taken aback. I never said that.

"Sorry, I'm not sure what you mean."

"Ye, ye commentating on the game!"

"Did you hear it, Alex?"

"No, no. I was told."

I explained what I'd said in the voiceover. I had to stand my corner. He didn't say sorry. But he did mellow.

"OK. What ye drinkin'?"

There was another time when I was at Old Trafford, and I almost lost my career. I got lucky. My blood still runs cold thinking about it.

I was there for The Match. A live Sunday game for ITV. The Doc's wife Jean was the PA. One of the crew down in London asked her if I could do a fifteen second promo for the game. No problem.

I was looking at an off-air monitor showing Granada TV. The cartoons were on. I had one eye on Daffy Duck. Jean asked me if I was ready. As the cartoons were still on, I thought it was only a rehearsal.

I started to mess about. I did the promo, but switched my accent into a broad Scouse one. Then back again. I could've said anything. It was just a rehearsal.

Then London called Jean:

"Thanks Jean, and tell Elton thanks too. That was fine."

I'd gone out live!

The cartoons were only on Granada. It was just a regional variation. Other parts of the country had heard my "rehearsal".

I shuddered.

Imagine if I'd have gone rogue:

"Yeah err, fuckin' great game coming up at Old Trafford."

I thought back to my Radio City days. A Canadian journalist called John Darby joined the newsroom. He was experienced in radio. His words from the 1970s came to mind.

"Never swear in front of a microphone, even if you think it's turned off."

I'm sure that was ingrained in my brain and saved me that day.

A few years earlier, I was doing a weekly live Saturday night football in the Match of the Day slot. My guests would rotate between Denis Tueart and Ray Clemence.

For whatever reason, towards the end of one show, my mind went blank.

As we were heading to the closing credits, I said to Tueart "Anything else, Denis?"

He was stumped. Not his fault.

I was braindead and signed off saying "Good Afternight".

I felt a right dickhead. Denis was very understanding. I just held my hands up and said "Sorry Den, I don't know what went wrong".

Sometimes when things don't go according to plan, I've been around to save the day. Like in 1985 when Everton played QPR. There was also another narrow escape when I was working on Midweek Sports Special, around the same period.

Brian Moore was presenting that night. Two minutes before going on air, Brian wanted to run through the opening again with the lady responsible for the autocue. She was just sat there, doing her knitting!

As Mooro was going through it, the autocue broke. It was really flimsy, like a piece of toilet roll in front of the lens. Mooro started to panic. I thought he was going to have a heart attack.

With seconds to spare, the autocue was fixed.

Secretly, I was a little disappointed.

37

The last word

If things had been different in 1962, I could've been a Liverpool fan. Being locked out for the game at Anfield led to me to Everton. That's a sliding doors moment in my life. I've had a fair few of them.

I might've been watching football for a very, very long time but there are still players that I never saw. If time travel were possible, these are the players I'd like to have seen. Was the hype all that it was cracked up to be?

Di Stefano and Puskas (Real Madrid), Didi (Brazil), Juste Fontaine (France), John Charles (Wales), Jim Baxter (Scotland), Peter Doherty (Northern Ireland), Stanley Matthews, Tom Finney and Duncan Edwards (England).

But above all, I'd like to get in my own personal Tardis and be transported back to 1927 for the 27/28 season when Everton's Bill (Dixie) Dean scored sixty league goals.

He must've been as good as we're told. To score so many headers when the balls absorbed mud and water was unbelievable. They were like medicine balls.

Dixie's milestone will never be emulated. Erling Haaland's 52 in all competitions was probably the closest we'll ever see. Just for the record, Dixie also scored three times in the FA Cup during that incredible season.

In total, in 433 Everton appearances, he scored 383 times. In modern day conditions, who knows what he might've achieved. It's true what they say about Dixie.

I was close to so many of the managers at Goodison. They were all different characters. Some like Colin Harvey, Joe Royle and Howard Kendall became friends. I went to two World Cups with Billy Bingham. Gordon Lee was...er...Gordon Lee.

You can't put a price on meeting and working with your childhood heroes, like Denis Law, Jimmy Greaves, George Best, Johan Cruyff and Everton's Holy Trinity. It's reputed to be disappointing.

Not in my case.

On one occasion, Joe Royle and I were in London and with a bit of time on our hands, I suggested we drop in to see Bestie at his club "Blondes".

We walked into the club and George was there with a couple of beauties. He began telling us of an incident when he was playing in America. He represented three different clubs over there. At this particular time, he hadn't had a drink for months. He'd been at an awards dinner where he'd been voted above the likes of Beckenbauer, Cruyff and Pelé as player of the year. What an honour.

"It was a great feeling. I felt on top of the world."

George was being driven back to wherever he was staying. Then Bestie saw a bar set back from the road. He told the driver to stop. George got out and was in the bar for about two days.

"It might've been shorter than that or even longer. I don't remember. That's when I realised there was no cure for my disease."

It got him in the end, but there was nothing he could do to prevent the inevitable. It's terribly sad. He arguably could've become the greatest if his career at the top level hadn't been cut short due to his lifestyle. He died aged 59.

Bestie's mate Denis Law was quick-witted. I once asked him about England's 1966 World Cup win.

"Didn't watch it. Played golf instead!"

Denis, forever the proud Scotsman!

Greavsie was hilarious. Anyone who saw him on TV in the 1980s and 1990s knows that. In today's climate, he'd never get away with the things he used to say. One lunchtime on Saint and Greavsie, he was talking to Ian about the Oxford and Cambridge boat race:

"What a strange sport it is. The winners dipping their cox in the river afterwards."

Delivered straight-faced, while Saint struggled to hold it together.

Great days.

Talking of which, Everton could do with bringing the good times back. We look a long way off from that. As we did in 1994. Although the following season, we won the FA Cup.

We'd avoided relegation by the narrowest of margins. Two nil down to Wimbledon at home and we were as good as down. But Everton scored three times and we were spared the ignominy of second-tier football for the 94/95 season. Manager Mike Walker didn't last and Joe Royle came from Oldham in November 1994. Big Joe was a breath of fresh air and he created a strong mentality. His midfield became known as "The Dogs of War".

As the cup run reached the quarter-final stage, my daughter Laura made her debut at Goodison Park. The match against Newcastle turned out to be extremely memorable for her.

Thanks to Cliff Finch, club chairman Peter Johnson's number two, we were sat in the directors box. Everyone made a fuss of Laura. Big Joe also said to bring her down to the dressing room after the game to meet the lads.

She was only ten.

Of course, to make it complete we needed to win. Skipper Dave Watson obliged with the game's only goal. Shortly after the final whistle, we made our way to the dressing room.

I knocked on the door and Mick "Baz" Rathbone answered.

"You're a bit early Elt. The lads haven't changed yet."

Next minute, a giant appeared in the doorway.

"Alright wee man, who's this?"

Laura meet Duncan Ferguson.

"Giz her 'ere, c'mon sweetheart."

Big Dunc picked her up and gave her a guided tour of a virtually naked dressing room. I wonder how many ten-year-old girls have been given such an eye opener.

It wasn't long before Joe brought her back to me. He's a family friend and he certainly came to the rescue that afternoon!

Tottenham were taken apart 4-1 in the semi-final at Elland Road, as a result of "the greatest substitution that I never made" according to Joe. Daniel Amokachi subbed himself on. And promptly scored two goals!

One year on from the relegation trapdoor, we were heading to Wembley, where a Paul Rideout goal won us our last piece of silverware.

I love the fact that my son Chris works with Richard Keys and Andy Gray. After my long history with both men, to see my son with them in Qatar is very gratifying. I wish I could join Chris and Andy on the golf course. Maybe they need a caddy! I certainly can't play.

Chris got into TV early on. In fact, much earlier than most.

We were doing a live game at Goodison Park between Everton and Arsenal in 1988. A big one too. The first leg of the League Cup semi-final. Bryan Robson was my guest. When the cameras were off us, ten-year-old Chris watched the game sat on Bryan's knee!

Chris later worked as a runner for Granada. Who gave him the opportunity? The Doc.

Paul Doherty died in 2016, aged 77. His funeral was held in the Bolton area.

I dreaded that day so much. What's more, I got lost and I was late. I've always been proud of my punctuality. As I sat in the church, I thought back to something Paul had once said:

"You'll be late for your own fucking funeral you!"

And there I was. Late for his.

The turnout was incredible. One of the mourners was Sir Alex. I'll leave it at that.

When I set out to write this book, I didn't want it to be a rags to riches story, because it isn't. I didn't have it hard as a kid. We didn't live in a one-up, one-down terrace house in St. Helens. I didn't share a tin bath with all the family. These types of books begin with stories like this. Not mine.

We had a nice house. That was the same wherever we lived. My dad was a bank manager and my mum a primary school teacher. You could say I had a privileged upbringing. When we moved to Liverpool, I was sent to private education.

Joyce and I divorced in the 1990s but we've stayed good friends. We probably get on better now than ever before. I love being a granddad. Laura's two boys, Dylan and Oscar are both football daft. Evertonians like me and their uncle Chris. Hopefully one day, they'll see what I've seen.

I was actually born in Lancaster. At a home for unmarried mothers. I was adopted by Ruth and Len. They'll always be my mum and dad. I miss them to this day.

I've known about being adopted for as long as I can remember. I was told when I was very young. It didn't bother me.

"Oh okay, what's for tea?"

My parents didn't have an "accident" or a faulty contraceptive, I was chosen. That's a special and enduring feeling. I hope all adoptees see it that way.

I've met my biological family. They're in Wales. I have three half-brothers and a half-sister on my biological mum's side. They're good people and I keep in touch with my half-brother Geraint.

That's how these books normally start. I thought I'd leave it to the end.

Now let's finish off with a laugh or two.

I was once prosecuted and banned from driving for being under the influence. I was leaving the golf club and swerved to avoid an oncoming vehicle that was travelling way too fast.

I drove into a fence.

Once I got home, I reported the incident to the police. Somewhat shaken, I tucked into a bottle of Scotch to settle my nerves. About two hours later, there's a knock on the door. It was a WPC. She asked me about the incident. I was breathalysed there and then and taken to the cop shop.

I went to court pleading innocence at the time of the altercation with the fence, but it didn't wash with the magistrates.

Fair enough. Live and learn. It even made front page of the Liverpool Echo.

Shortly afterwards, I was speaking at a function with Stan Boardman. I should've known what was coming.

"Elton's here, you probably all know he's been done for drink driving.

In court he asked for six other fences to be taken into consideration."

Brilliant Stan!

Right, as Sir Trevor McDonald used to say:

"And finally..."

One Saturday, due to technical issues at LWT, we presented the Results Service from the ITN studios.

It came right after the news. So I was sat next to Trevor McDonald. This was before his knighthood.

He concluded the news:

"Coming up after the break, Elton Welsby with all of today's football news."

What a nice man too. He explained how things might be slightly different working in a strange studio. The differences were minor and there was nothing really to worry about. Bob Patience was producing as always, so all in all it was business as usual.

So as not to make a fuss, Sir Trevor stayed for my fifteen-minute slot. He remarked how I didn't use autocue. I explained how things would change as the programme progressed, so autocue would be a hindrance rather than helpful.

He appreciated that. As he departed, he said to me:

"Well done, that's not my idea of fun."

It was to me though, Sir Trevor!

I can't finish the book without mentioning Fred the Weatherman.

Fred Talbot and I were colleagues at Granada. Fred was openly gay and that was fine with all of us. We had no idea he was a paedophile. He was subsequently jailed for his crimes against under-age boys during his teaching days.

On the face of it, Fred was okay.

When ITV's This Morning came from the Albert Dock in Liverpool, presented by Richard and Judy, Fred was very popular, as he hopped across a floating map to forecast the weather.

One night at a function in Kirkby, Liverpool, a comedian was taking the piss out of the well-known Granada presenters. He joked that Fred and I were an item.

Well, that rumour swept around Merseyside like you wouldn't believe.

So I used it in my after-dinner speeches.

I'd start by saying "Gentlemen I'd like to confirm three things.

1) I am standing up.

2) My full name is Roger Elton Welsby.

That's what I was christened.

AND

3) I am not shagging Fred the Weatherman!!

Cue the audience.

Standing ovation.

The only time it got a bit nasty was when I was at home and discovered a News of the World "journalist" parked at the end of the driveway.

"Is there any truth in these stories about you and Fred Talbot?"

I laughed and said, quite simply, no.

At that moment my daughter, Laura, was being dropped off from school.

The journo said "Mr Welsby, are you a homosexual?"

Laura didn't hear what she'd said, nor did she hear my reply.

Pinching a line off Bernard Manning, I replied:

"Look love, if every bird looked like you we'd all be homosexuals.

Now FUCK OFF!!"

She did.

No such story ever appeared in the News of the World.

So that's it. I've told you everything. Except Roger Black's risqué joke. Maybe when I'm doing a book signing, I'll tell you.

If nothing else…

I'm game for a laugh!

Printed in Great Britain
by Amazon